COLLECTIONS

Teacher's Edition
Practice Book
Grade 1

Welcome Home

Set Sail

Harcourt

Orlando   Boston   Dallas   Chicago   San Diego

Visit *The Learning Site!*
www.harcourtschool.com

ISBN 0-15-312719-8

3 4 5 6 7 8 9 10   059   2002   2001   2000

Contents

WELCOME HOME

Contents

SET SAIL

Contents

Welcome
Home

Name _____

▶ **Look at each picture. Write the word in the box that completes the sentence.**

| green | bee | eat | seat | me | feet |

1. The cat is on the _____ seat _____.

2. She sees the _____ bee _____.

3. She lands on her _____ feet _____.

4. She wants to _____ eat _____.

5. Her rug is _____ green _____.

6. She comes to _____ me _____.

Welcome Home
Lesson 1

 SCHOOL-HOME CONNECTION Write the words. Ask your child to circle the words with *ee* and to draw a line under the words with *ea*. Then let him or her read the words.

Harcourt

Name _____

▶ **Write the name of the holiday that matches each clue. Begin each holiday name with a capital letter.**

valentine's day	new year's day	thanksgiving day

I. We make cards for friends. We use red.

_____

Valentine's Day

2. This is the first day of the year!

_____

New Year's Day

3. We give thanks this day.

_____

Thanksgiving Day

TRY THIS Write about your favorite holiday. Draw a picture to go with your story.

SCHOOL–HOME CONNECTION Look at a calendar with your child.
Review the holidays and special days for each month.

Welcome Home
Lesson 1

9

Harcourt

Name ______________________________

▶ **Write the word that best completes each sentence.**

full	should	room	Try	moved

Cat came into the ___room___. I ___moved___ her bowl down. Her dish was ___full___. "You ___should___ eat," I said. "It's good. ___Try___ some."

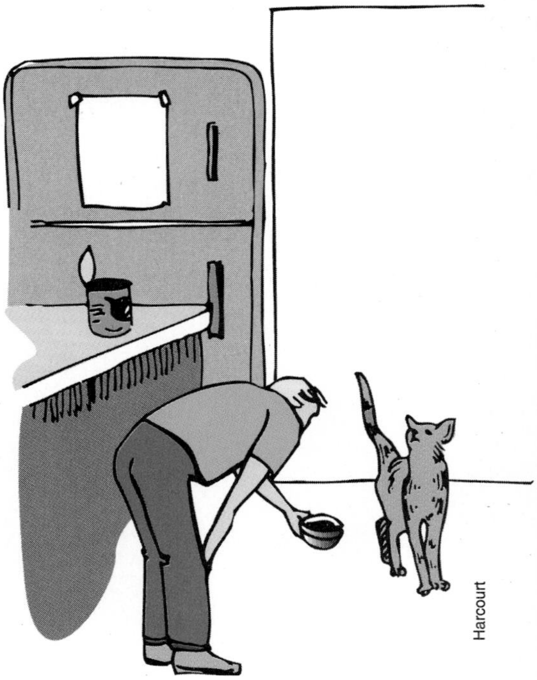

Name _____

▶ **Write the word that best completes each sentence.**

| hear | only | Please | write | full |

Now my cat is _____ full _____ .

I _____ hear _____ her. She is happy.

She likes it. I _____ write _____ "yes."

" _____ Please _____ get more for my cat."

If _____ only _____ she liked all

her food.

TRY THIS Use some of the words from the box to write a note to a friend. Then circle the words you picked.

SCHOOL-HOME CONNECTION Ask your child to read each sentence of the story.

Welcome Home
Lesson 2

11

Harcourt

Name _____

▶ **Do what each sentence tells you. Then circle the words that contain vowel ē.**

1. A cat (eats) a (sweet) (treat). Color the ice (cream).
2. One cat (feels) the (heat). Color this cat pink.
3. A (teeny) cat (sees) the fish. Color this cat (green).
4. The cat (cleans) its (feet). Color this cat yellow.
5. (Three) cats (seem) tired. They want to (sleep).
   Color them red.
6. A cat (reads) to me. Color its (feet).

Harcourt

SCHOOL-HOME CONNECTION Write the long vowel *e* words in the sentences on small cards. Have your child read the words and catergorize them according to the spelling (*e, ee, ea*).

Name _____

► **Write the spelling word in the box that tells about the picture.**

| we | see | eat | read | me |

1.

_____

- - - - - - - - - - - - - - - - - -

me or see

2.

_____

- - - - - - - - - - - - - - - - - -

eat

3.

_____

- - - - - - - - - - - - - - - - - -

we or see

4.

_____

- - - - - - - - - - - - - - - - - -

read

5.

_____

- - - - - - - - - - - - - - - - - -

see or we

Harcourt

SCHOOL-HOME CONNECTION Cut out 14 small squares. Write one letter on each square: 6 *e*'s, 2 *a*'s, 1 *w*, 1 *s*, 1 *t*, 1 *d*, 1 *m*, and 1 *r*. Then turn them over and take turns picking a letter until you can make a spelling word.

Welcome Home
Lesson 2   **13**

Name _____

▶ **Think about what happened in the story.**
Then complete the flowchart. Responses may vary.

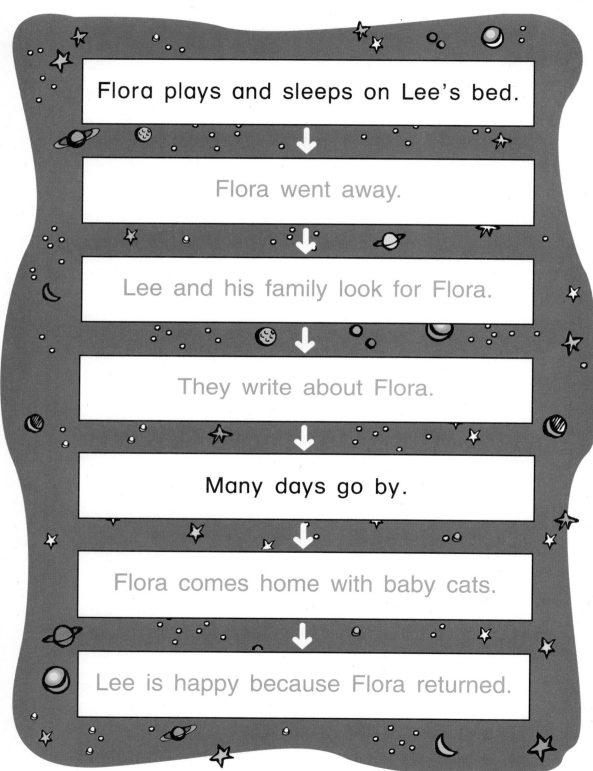

Flora plays and sleeps on Lee's bed.

⬇

Flora went away.

⬇

Lee and his family look for Flora.

⬇

They write about Flora.

⬇

Many days go by.

⬇

Flora comes home with baby cats.

⬇

Lee is happy because Flora returned.

SCHOOL-HOME CONNECTION Have your child retell the
story, using the flowchart to tell the events in order.

Harcourt

▶ **Draw a picture to show what happens next.** Accept reasonable responses.

 TRY THIS Write sentences to go with your story.

SCHOOL-HOME CONNECTION Ask your child to tell you a story about the pictures.

Harcourt

Name _____

▶ **Look at the pictures. Then choose the best answer. Fill in the oval next to your answer.**

1. What will happen next?

  ⊝ Snow will fall.

  ⊝ The man will play.

  ⊜ The snow will melt.

  ⊝ The man will grow.

▶ **Choose the best answer. Fill in the circle next to your answer.**

2. What will happen next?

  ⊜ He will get a haircut.

  ⊝ He will eat lunch.

  ⊝ He will read a book.

  ⊝ He will brush his teeth.

Harcourt

Name _____

▶ **Write the word that best completes each sentence.**

flying   flies

_____

----

1. She _____flies_____ away and comes back.

hunting   hunts

_____

----

2. She _____hunts_____ for soft

things to pad the nest.

carry   carries

_____

----

3. She _____carries_____ them

back to the nest.

tried   trying

_____

----

4. She _____tried_____ to make

a good nest.

SCHOOL-HOME CONNECTION Together, write a list of words that end in -s, -ed, and -es. Take turns making up a sentence with each word.

Welcome Home
Lesson 5   **17**

Harcourt

Name _____

▶ **Use the word from the box that best completes each sentence. Then read the story.**

| Take | cake | gave | Kate | game | ate |

The Surprise

_____ Kate _____ is my friend. She _____ gave _____

me a map. "_____ Take _____ this map, and find the

surprise." I walked all around the house.

The _____ game _____ was fun. The surprise

was a birthday _____ cake _____.

We _____ ate _____ it all!

SCHOOL-HOME CONNECTION Read the words in the box. Ask your child to write *gave*, *game*, and *ate*. Then write two rhyming words for each.

Harcourt

Name _____

▶ **Read the story and complete the
sentences with the words I or me.**

_____I_____ like to go to the park with Doug. We

swing. Doug pushes ___me___. Then ___I___ push

him. We play ball. ___I___ kick the ball to Doug. He

kicks the ball to ___me___. We climb. ___I___ go up to

the top. ___I___ like to play at the park.

SCHOOL-HOME CONNECTION Ask your child to draw a picture of himself
or herself playing with a friend. Have your child write a caption using *I*.
Then have your child write a second caption using *me*.

Welcome Home
Lesson 6   **19**

Name _____

▶ **Choose the word from the box that best completes each sentence.**

world	place	country	Earth	town
special		United States of America		

1. My room is a _____special_____ place.

2. The _____Earth_____ spins around the sun.

3. The flag of the _____United States_____

_____of America_____ has stars and stripes.

4. What _____country_____ do you live in?

Harcourt

Name _____

▶ **Read each clue. Write the word that solves the riddle.**

5. It is shaped like a ball. People live here. It's also called Earth.

world

6. Some people call it U.S.A. for short.

United States of America

7. It's not the biggest place to live. People live, work, and shop here. It sounds like <u>down</u>.

town

8. I am somewhere. I sound like <u>space</u>.

place

TRY THIS Write the vocabulary words on separate pieces of paper. Put the words in order, from shortest to longest.

SCHOOL–HOME CONNECTION Talk to your child about the names of your street, town, state, and country. Ask your child to address an envelope to themselves. Write him or her a special note and mail it.

Harcourt

Name _____

▶ **Use the words in the box. Write the word that names the picture.**

| shade | skate | lake | wave | grapes |

1.  _____
   lake

2.  _____
   wave

3.  _____
   shade

4.  _____
   grapes

5.  _____
   skate

Welcome Home
Lesson 7

SCHOOL-HOME CONNECTION Ask your child to make a list of the words in the box. Color the *a*'s yellow. Color the *e*'s green. Circle each letter between. Read the words and talk about the pattern.

Harcourt

Name _____

▶ **Write the word that best completes each sentence.**

came	game	made	make	take

1. Come play a _____game_____ with us.

2. We need to _____make_____ a team.

3. We _____came_____ to give you a map.

4. We _____made_____ it.

5. It is faster if you _____take_____ the bus.

TRY THIS Write a two-line poem about soccer. Use one or two spelling words.

SCHOOL-HOME CONNECTION Make pairs of words that sound the same. Add two more rhyming words to each pair.

▶ **Think about the story. Think about the maps and the places on the maps. Write the places in order to complete the story chart.**

Possible responses are given.

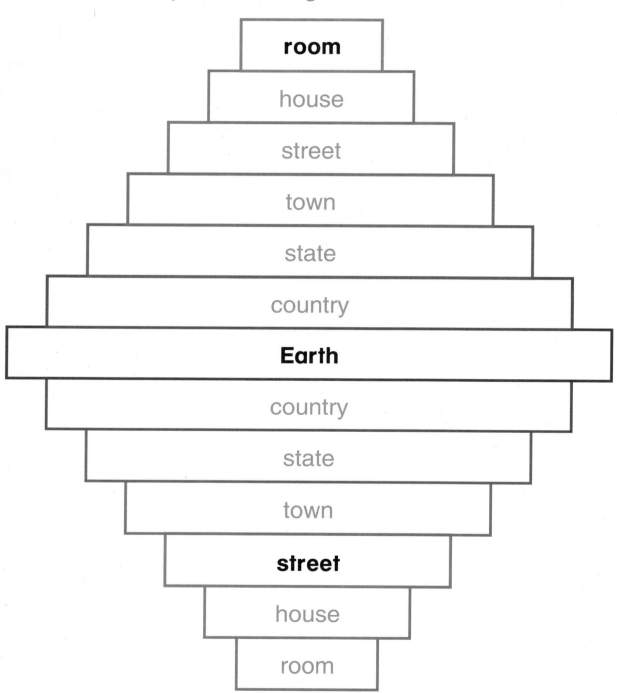

room
house
street
town
state
country

Earth

country
state
town

street

house
room

SCHOOL-HOME CONNECTION Help your child draw a map of his or her bedroom. Help your child label it and write his or her address on the other side.

Harcourt

▶ **Look at Joey's picture and story. Write the word in the box that best completes each sentence.**

| sleeps | neat | clean | me | green | She |

See _____ me _____ in my room? I can

_____ clean _____ my room. I like it _____ neat _____.

I have a _____ green _____ door. My dog

_____ sleeps _____ in my room. _____ She _____

likes the soft rug.

SCHOOL-HOME CONNECTION Write the words as a list. Talk about the letters that stand for the long *e* sound. Let your child circle the *e*, *ee*, or *ea* in each word. Think of other long *e* words and write them.

Harcourt

Name _____

▶ **Read the story. Then answer the question.**

    This is a map of the United States. It is a big country. It has many towns. There are 50 states. People live and work in every state. There is much to see in the United States.

What is this story about?

_____

It is about the United States.

_____

_____

Harcourt

SCHOOL-HOME CONNECTION Tell your child a story about a move you made. Ask him or her to draw a picture of your story.

▶ **Read each story. Then choose the best answer. Fill in the oval next to your answer.**

Owls are night birds. Some are big and some are small. They hunt at night. They catch mice and small animals. They sleep in the day.

1. What is this story about?
    - ⬭ It is about mice.
    - ⬭ It is about night.
    - ⬤ It is about owls.
    - ⬭ It is about sleep.

Many animals hatch from eggs. Birds and ducks hatch from eggs. Frogs and snakes hatch from eggs. Bugs hatch from eggs, too.

2. What is this story about?
    - ⬭ It is about bugs.
    - ⬭ It is about ducks.
    - ⬭ It is about animals that swim.
    - ⬤ It is about animals that hatch.

Name _____

▶ **Write the word that best completes each sentence.**

made	late	came	gave	take

1. I _____ made _____ a map.

2. I will _____ take _____ my map with me.

3. Jenny _____ came _____ with me.

4. We can't be _____ late _____!

5. We _____ gave _____ our maps to Mr. Smith.

TRY THIS Make a list of words with the ending -ake. Compare your list with a partner.

SCHOOL-HOME CONNECTION Help your child write five new sentences using each word from the box above. Ask him or her to circle the vocabulary word in each sentence.

Harcourt

Name _____

▶ **Look at the picture. Follow the directions to finish the picture.** Be sure children complete the picture.

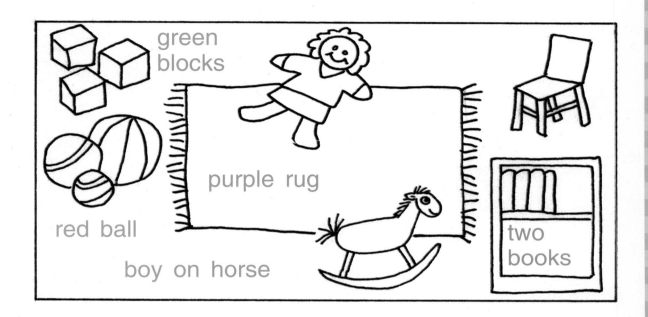

green blocks

purple rug

red ball

boy on horse

two books

1. Color the blocks green.

2. Make two more books on the shelf.

3. Put a boy on the horse.

4. Color the rug purple.

5. Color one ball red.

 TRY THIS Draw a picture for a friend. Write a sentence that tells your friend to do something to your picture. Watch your friend follow your directions.

Harcourt

 SCHOOL-HOME CONNECTION Give your child a blank sheet of paper and a crayon. Give one direction, like *"draw a big circle"* or *"fold the paper in half."* Then you take the paper, and let your child give you a direction.

Welcome Home
Lesson 9   **29**

▶ **Read Ann's list. Circle the words that sound like <u>cake</u>.**

1. Cut apples to (make) a pie.

2. (Bake) the pie.

3. Go outside and (shake) the rug.

4. (Take) out the trash.

▶ **Draw a line under the words that sound like <u>late</u>.**

5. Open the <u>gate</u>.

6. Get a <u>plate</u> for each of us.

7. Call <u>Kate</u> to come.

8. Then eat the pie and go <u>skate</u> with <u>Kate</u>!

 TRY THIS Make a list of the words that end with <u>ake</u>. Then make a list of the words that end with <u>ate</u>.

SCHOOL-HOME CONNECTION Ask your child to pick two words that rhyme from this page. Together, write a two-line poem.

Harcourt

Name _____

▶ **Read the story. Circle the words with y or ie.**

This (tiny) spot on the map is our town. We are having a town birthday. Today the town is 100 years old. We are (busy.) We play games and tell (stories.) We eat (pie) and cake. We read (very) old newspapers. (Everybody) is (happy) because our town is (really) special.

SCHOOL-HOME CONNECTION With your child, make a list of the circled words. Read each word and have your child circle the y's and the ie's.

Welcome Home
Lesson 11

31

Name _____

▶ **Use a word from the box to complete each sentence. Circle the noun that the new word tells about.**

| They | he | She | it |

1. Is (Tom) home?

_____

Can _____he_____ play with us?

2. Does Tom have a (bat)?

_____

He can bring _____it_____ to play ball.

3. (Bill and Pam) are coming, too.

_____

_____They_____ will meet us at the park.

4. (Mother) will bring us home.

_____

_____She_____ can bring Tom home, too.

SCHOOL-HOME CONNECTION Write a sentence for your child. Read it aloud. Ask your child to change the noun to *he, she, it,* or *they,* and say the sentence again. Repeat to use each of the pronouns.

Harcourt

Name _____

▶ **Read the words in the box. Match each word to a clue. Write the word.**

| before | thought | nice | laugh | most | carry |

It's more than some.

_____

most

I did think about it.

_____

thought

Take it with you.

_____

carry

You do this for fun.

_____

laugh

I am not mean.

_____

nice

Not today, but yesterday.

_____

before

TRY THIS Use words in the box to write three sentences. Then draw pictures to match your sentences.

Harcourt

Name _____

▶ **Read the words in the box. Write the word that completes the sentence.**

thought	nice	laugh	most	carry

1. I _____carry_____ a new book to my brother.

2. He is very _____nice_____.

3. We play _____most_____ of the time.

4. We _____laugh_____ at the story.

5. We _____thought_____ the book was very good.

TRY THIS Write the word <u>nice</u>. Write a sentence with this word. Then draw a picture to go with your sentence.

SCHOOL-HOME CONNECTION Let your child pick out a favorite story book. Read it together.

Harcourt

▶ **Read the paragraph. Find the words that have the long vowel e sound spelled y or ie. Circle them. Then write the words below.**

Most of the time my (baby) sister (Katie) is (happy). I showed her how to sort blocks. She does it (quickly) now. When she's (really) (hungry), she cries. That's what (babies) do best!

baby	quickly
Katie	really
happy	hungry
	babies

SCHOOL-HOME CONNECTION With your child, review the list. Have your child draw a line around the letters that stand for the long e sound

Welcome Home
Lesson 12

35

Harcourt

Name _____

▶ **Write the word in the box that best completes the sentence.**

any	Katie	many	very	funny

LIBRARY

1. I have _____ many _____ books to read.

2. Some books are _____ very _____ big.

3. I read to _____ Katie _____.

4. Some stories are really _____ funny _____.

5. I do not have _____ any _____ books left.

SCHOOL-HOME CONNECTION Read picture books together, and try to find these spelling words on the pages.

Harcourt

Name _____

▶ **Think about Lilly's feelings during the
story. Then complete the flowchart.** Answers will vary.

1. Lilly is happy to
see Katie.

2. She is sad when
Mommy and
Daddy leave.

3. She is happy
to eat.

4. She misses Mommy
and Daddy.

5. She is silly at
the park.

6. She sees men
playing ball
and misses
Daddy.

7. She is happy to see
Mommy and
Daddy.

8. She cries for
Katie.

TRY THIS Add a new part to the story. Write about a few more
ups and downs in Lilly's day.

 SCHOOL-HOME CONNECTION Help your child write or
draw a story sequence about an imaginary day when he
or she has ups and downs.

▶ **Use the words in the box. Write the word that best completes each sentence.**

garden	park	cart	car	yarn

1. I go with Mom and Dad in the _____ car _____ .

2. We _____ park _____ the car.

3. We get a _____ cart _____ .

4. Mom gets red _____ yarn _____ .

5. Here is a plant for the _____ garden _____ .

TRY THIS Make a list of words that contain <u>ar</u>. Are the letters at the beginning, the end, or in the middle of the words?

SCHOOL-HOME CONNECTION Ask your child to read the words in the box. Have him or her circle the two letters that are the same in every word and then read the words again.

Harcourt

Name _____

▶ **Read the story. Then answer the questions.** Answers will vary.

Jack and his mother go to the beach. They walk on the hot sand. They get wet. They find small shells. They write in the sand. The beach is a nice place to play.

Main Idea
What is the story about?
The beach is a nice place for Jack and his mother.

↓

Details
What did you find out?
Jack and his mother walk on the sand.
They get wet.
They find shells.
They write in the sand.

TRY THIS Draw a picture of yourself at the beach or at a pool. Label five details in your picture.

Harcourt

SCHOOL-HOME CONNECTION Talk about a recent trip you took with your child. Recall some of the details.

Welcome Home
Lesson 13   **39**

Name _____

▶ **Read each story. Then choose the best answer. Fill in the oval next to your answer.**

Lilly saw a kangaroo. The kangaroo had a baby with her. The baby kangaroo was brown and had a long tail. It could jump fast and far.

1. What did you learn about the kangaroo?

   ⬭ It is small.

   ⬬ It can jump far.

   ⬭ It has long arms.

   ⬭ It has a short tail.

Apples grow on trees. Apples can be green, red, or yellow. Some are sweet. Some are tart. Some are good to bake with. Others are better for eating fresh. Apples are ready to pick in the fall.

2. What did you learn about apples?

   ⬭ Apples are always red.

   ⬭ Apples are good in soup.

   ⬭ Apple seeds are good to eat.

   ⬬ You can bake some apples.

Harcourt

Name _____

▶ **Write the words in ABC order. One has been done for you in each set.**

laugh yell pick duck

1. ___duck___

2. ___laugh___

3. ___pick___

4. ___yell___

  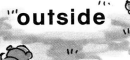

baby happy outside walk

1. ___baby___

2. ___happy___

3. ___outside___

4. ___walk___

SCHOOL-HOME CONNECTION Write each of these words on a small card. Let your child pick three and put them in ABC order. Mix them and play again.

Harcourt

Name _____

▶ **Read each sentence. Combine the two words to form a contraction. Write the contraction to complete the sentence.**

She is
_____

1. _____She's_____ getting lots of nuts.

He is
_____

2. _____He's_____ busy, too.

do not
_____

3. They _____don't_____ eat them all now.

They will
_____

4. _____They'll_____ put the nuts away.

SCHOOL-HOME CONNECTION Make a list of these contractions with your child. Next to each contraction, ask your child to write the two words that make up the contraction.

Harcourt

▶ **Write the word in the box that best completes each sentence in the story.**

| feet | sweet | meet | feed |

I _____ meet _____ Mitch

every Monday. We like to get our

_____ feet _____ wet in the pond. We like to

_____ feed _____ the ducks. On the way home

we get a _____ sweet _____ treat.

SCHOOL-HOME CONNECTION Ask your child which words rhyme with *need*.

Welcome Home
Lesson 15

43

Harcourt

Name _____

► **Solve each riddle. Write the words in the puzzle.**

five	bike	smile	white	slide	time

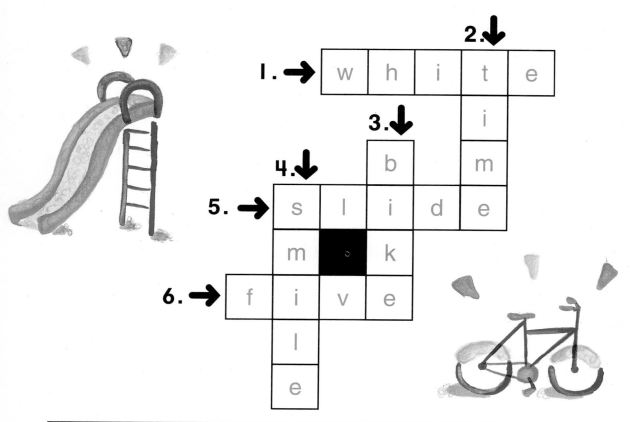

1.	the color of snow
2.	use a clock to tell _ _ _ _
3.	two-wheeler
4.	seen on a happy face
5.	ride down the _ _ _ _ _
6.	5

Welcome Home
Lesson 16

SCHOOL-HOME CONNECTION Have your child
write a rhyming word for each word in the puzzle.

Harcourt

Name _____

▶ **Look at the pictures and write a word that describes the feeling.**

happy	hungry	sad	surprised	tired

1. _____ sad _____

2. _____ surprised _____

3. _____ happy _____

4. _____ tired _____

5. _____ hungry _____

SCHOOL-HOME CONNECTION With your child, think of other words that describe feelings. Have your child draw a picture of one new word.

Welcome Home
Lesson 16

45

Harcourt

Name _____

▶ **Write the word that completes each sentence. Read the story when you are finished.**

My Fishing Story

gone   together
_____

1. Dad and I fish _____together_____.

once   sound
_____

2. We like the _____sound_____ of the water.

sound   while
_____

3. I whistle _____while_____ I fish.

Once   While
_____

4. _____Once_____ I saw lots of fish.

gone   bears
_____

5. We saw two _____bears_____ fishing for food.

Harcourt

Name _____

▶ **Write the word that completes each sentence. Read the story when you are finished.**

sorry   gone
_____

1. I am _____ sorry _____ I forgot our snack.

---

while   together
_____

2. We get hungry _____ while _____ we fish.

Bears   Once
_____

3. _____ Once _____ we are home,

we will eat fish.

---

sound   bears
_____

4. The _____ bears _____ will eat fish, too!

TRY THIS Write a sentence for the word <u>together</u>. Then draw a picture to go with your sentence.

SCHOOL-HOME CONNECTION Read this story together. Talk about food you like to eat and where it comes from.

Welcome Home
Lesson 17

47

Harcourt

► **Read the story. Circle the words that have the same vowel sound as in <u>mine</u>. Then write each word on the chart.**

Bear's Find

Bear sees a bee (hive) in a (pine) tree. He will go up the (side) of the tree. In a little (while) he will have lunch. The sweet treat will be (fine.) We (like) this lunch, but the bees are not (nice.)

1. _hive_	2. _fine_
3. _pine_	4. _like_
5. _side_	6. _nice_
7. _while_	

TRY THIS

Put all the <u>i-e</u> words in alphabetical order.

SCHOOL-HOME CONNECTION Make twelve letter cards with your child. Put one letter on each card: *i, e, h, v, p, n, l, e, s, d, k* and *c*. Use the letters to make a list of *i-e* words.

Harcourt

Name _____

► **Read the questions. Circle the answers.**

1. What is six plus three?

   time   (nine)

2. What sometimes has two wheels?

   (bike)   like

3. What do you do on a bus or in a car?

   (ride)   nine

4. What do you want to know when you look
   at a clock?

   bike   (time)

5. How do you feel about a friend?

   ride   (like)

TRY THIS Draw a picture for one of the spelling words.
Write the word under your picture.

SCHOOL-HOME CONNECTION Ask your child to write each
word he or she circled. Then circle the pair of rhyming words.

Welcome Home
Lesson 17   49

Harcourt

Name _____

 ▶ **Think about the story. Then fill in the story chart.** Responses may vary.

| **Title of the Story** Splash! |  **The Main Characters** Sam and Nelly |

Beginning
Sam and Nelly wake up.

Middle
They run to the river, but the bears aren't happy about their coming.

Ending
They fish with the bears until they are full. Then they take a nap.

Harcourt

 TRY THIS Change the ending of the story. Write a new ending and draw a picture about it.

SCHOOL-HOME CONNECTION Ask your child to tell the story of Sam and Nelly. Talk about hibernation and the animals that hibernate.

Name _____

▶ **Read the poem. Circle all the words that have the /ā/ sound spelled *a-e*. Write the words on the chart.**

I play in a (wave,)
I hide in a (cave.)
I (race) and play
A (game) all day.
I (make) my bed.
I'm always fed.
I (take) time to rest.
My home is the best!

_____ - - - - - - - wave _____	_____ - - - - - - - game _____
_____ - - - - - - - cave _____	_____ - - - - - - - make _____
_____ - - - - - - - race _____	_____ - - - - - - - take _____

TRY THIS Pick two words. Use them to write one sentence.
Draw a line under each word you use.

 SCHOOL-HOME CONNECTION Read the words on the chart. Talk about the letter pattern CVC*e*. Think of other words with this pattern and write them on your own chart.

Welcome Home
Lesson 18   51

Harcourt

Name _____

▶ **Draw a picture to show what happens next. Write a sentence about your picture.**

Responses may vary.

1. The boy plays in the water.

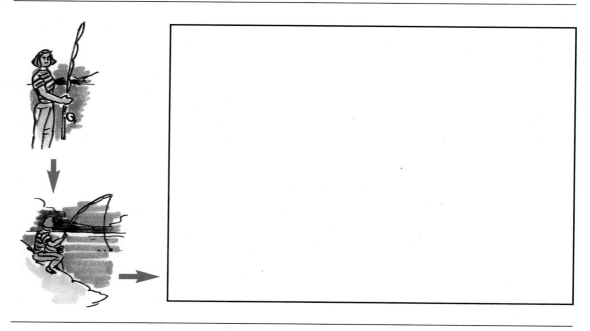

2. The girl has a fish.

Welcome Home
Lesson 18

SCHOOL-HOME CONNECTION Ask your child to tell you each story. Read aloud his or her sentence.

Harcourt

Name _____

▶ **Read the sentences. Write the word that matches each letter shape and makes sense.**

When	wheels	whale	Where	Why

1. W h e r e

are you going?

2. W h y   does the   w h a l e

have   w h e e l s ?

3. W h e n   I race, this will go fast.

TRY THIS Draw two real things that have wheels. Write a sentence about each picture.

SCHOOL-HOME CONNECTION Talk with your child about whales. Together, write a whale fact and draw a picture to go with it.

Harcourt

Name _____

▶ **Write the word from the box that names each picture.**

bike	lake	cake	rake

1. _____ lake

2. _____ cake

3. _____ bike

4. _____ rake

 TRY THIS Use the words to make two lists, one with <u>-ake</u> words and one with <u>-ike</u> words. Add two more words to each list.

SCHOOL-HOME CONNECTION Read the lists of words. Say each word, and ask your child to spell it aloud.

Harcourt

Name _____

▶ **Write the word that best completes each sentence.**

| city | space | ice | mice | nice |

1. A _____ city _____ is a busy place.

2. Did the _____ ice _____ melt yet?

3. I want to blast into _____ space _____.

4. I eat fish. What do _____ mice _____ eat?

5. My friends are _____ nice _____.

TRY THIS Fold a piece of paper into four squares. Use four words from the box. Write one word on each square and draw a picture about each word.

SCHOOL-HOME CONNECTION Write the word *space*. Talk about the sound that *s* and *c* stand for. Circle all the letters on the page that sound like *s*.

Welcome Home
Lesson 21

Harcourt

Name _____

▶ **Read the ad. Then follow the directions.**

1. Find two color words. Color each.

2. Find two words that tell about size. Put a line under each.

3. Find a word that tells about shape. Circle it.

Fred's Fish Shop

Come to my big shop. I have small fish for your tank. Take home a red fish or a yellow fish. I have round fish. Fish are fun!

TRY THIS Look around the classroom. Draw something you see. Write four describing words about it. Use words that tell about size, shape, and color.

SCHOOL-HOME CONNECTION Make a chart with three columns, one for color words, one for size words, and one for shape words. With your child, add words to each column.

Harcourt

▶ **Read the clues. Then write the matching words in the crossword puzzle.**

new ride pretty heard children school almost

1.	Not quite.
2.	A place to study.
3.	Do this on a bus.
4.	Looks nice.
5.	Rhymes with <u>bird</u>.
6.	Means the same as <u>kids</u>.
7.	It's not old.

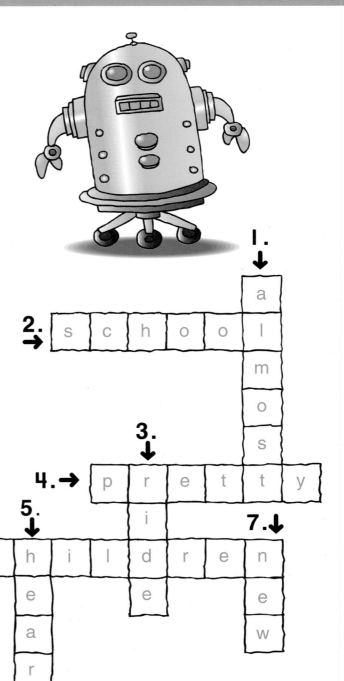

1. ↓

2. → s c h o o l
a
l
m
o
s

3. ↓
4. → p r e t t y
i

5. ↓
6. → c h i l d r e n
h e
e w
a
r
d

7. ↓
n
e
w

Harcourt

▶ **Write the word that best completes each sentence.**

almost   ride   heard   School

1. We | h | e | a | r | d | the bus.

2. | S | c | h | o | o | l | is not far away.

3. He does not | r | i | d | e | .

4. He | a | l | m | o | s | t | lost his hat.

 TRY THIS List all the vocabulary words that have an <u>o</u>. Make another list of all the vocabulary words with an <u>e</u>. Are any words on both lists?

 **SCHOOL-HOME CONNECTION** Ask your child to write other sentences for the vocabulary words. Then ask him or her to read the sentences.

Name _____

► **Write the word that tells about the picture on the computer screen.**

whisper	whirl	wheel	when

1.

_____

whisper

2.

_____

whirl

3.

_____

when

4.

_____

wheel

TRY THIS Use each word in a sentence. Write the sentences.

 SCHOOL-HOME CONNECTION Use four small cards. With your child, write one word on each card. On the other side of the card, write a riddle for the word. Share your riddles with a friend.

Harcourt

Name _____

▶ **Write the word from the box that best matches the clue.**

| race | face | dance | mice | nice |

1. It's fun to hear the song and move to the beat.

    dance

2. This can be happy or sad.

    face

3. Someone kind and good.

    nice

4. A chance to test your skill.

    race

5. Small animals with long tails.

    mice

SCHOOL-HOME CONNECTION Write each spelling word on a card. Match the rhyming words. Then spell them aloud.

Harcourt

▶ **Think about the story. Write your answers in the box.** Responses will vary.

Things Cecil Can Do

play games
help teacher
lead the band
ride home
do tricks
make cakes
mow grass
clean room

▶ **Finish the sentence.**

Cecil is best at _____ being a good friend. _____

_____

_____

SCHOOL-HOME CONNECTION Ask your child to tell you about the story. Talk about real machines that help you at home.

Welcome Home
Lesson 22   61

Harcourt

Name _____

▶ **Look at the pictures and draw what happens next. Then write a sentence about your picture.** Possible response is given.

The boy will feed the bird.

 SCHOOL-HOME CONNECTION Make up a three-part story. Tell the first two parts and have your child complete the third part. Repeat with a second story.

Harcourt

Name _____

▶ **Help the children line up in ABC order by their first names. Write their names in ABC order.**

| Todd | Russ | Dan | Jenny |

1. _____ Dan _____   2. _____ Jenny _____

_____   _____

3. _____ Russ _____   4. _____ Todd _____

▶ **Line up the children's robots in ABC order. Write their names in ABC order.**

| Wiz | Buzz | Zap | Fizz |

1. _____ Buzz _____   2. _____ Fizz _____

_____   _____

3. _____ Wiz _____   4. _____ Zap _____

Harcourt

SCHOOL-HOME CONNECTION Write all eight names on small cards. With your child, put all the names in ABC order.

Name _____

▶ **Circle the word that names the picture.**
Write the word.

1.    (face)
space

_____ face _____

2.    rice
(mice)

_____ mice _____

3.    (space)
trace

_____ space _____

4.    mice
(rice)

_____ rice _____

5.   (trace)
space

_____ trace _____

TRY THIS Cut out five squares. Write a clue for each word on the square. Write the answer word on the back. Give your clues to a friend to guess.

SCHOOL-HOME CONNECTION Ask your child to find three words on the page that rhyme. Think of other words that rhyme with them.

Harcourt

Name _____

▶ **Read the chart. Then write the contraction that completes each sentence.**

She is	She's
he is	he's
do not	don't
can not	can't
I will	I'll

1. Kate is tired. ____She's____ going to bed.

2. The robot can move, but it ____can't____ eat.

3. I want some cake. ____I'll____ make it.

4. Jack is late, but ____he's____ coming.

5. I ____don't____ have a red hat.

SCHOOL-HOME CONNECTION Read the sentences with your child.
Discuss item number 1. Ask your child to identify who is meant by
the word *she's*. Discuss the word *he's* in number four.

Name _____

▶ **Read each sentence. Look at the red words in each sentence. Write the word that means the opposite of the red word.**

rest	last	best	must	fast

1. My robot won **first** place. _____ last

2. When is the weather **worst** ? _____ best

3. Some people **work** outside. _____ rest

4. Some robots are **slow**. _____ fast

5. You **do not have to** march. _____ must

SCHOOL-HOME CONNECTION Use the words in the box. Pick a word and have your child use it in a sentence. Repeat for all the words.

Harcourt

Name _____

▶ **Draw a picture to go with each
sentence.**

Responses will vary.

The clown has a
purple wig.

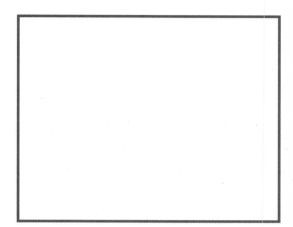

This clown has
a frown.

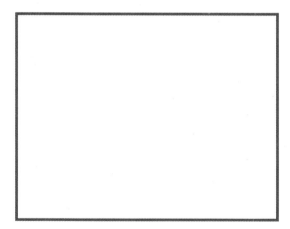

This clown has
a crown.

A clown has a
brown umbrella.

TRY THIS Read each sentence again. Circle all the words that
rhyme with <u>down</u>.

Harcourt

SCHOOL-HOME CONNECTION Draw a picture with your child of
a brown cow downtown. Write a sentence to go with the picture.

Name _____

▶ **Read the chart. Write the word in the box that best completes each sentence.**

Taste words	Smell words	Sound words	Feel words
sweet sour	fresh moldy	loud quiet	cold hot

1. is _____ cold _____.

2. A  is _____ sweet _____.

3. A is _____ sour _____.

4. Hot  smells _____ fresh _____.

5. A  is _____ loud _____.

SCHOOL-HOME CONNECTION Add one more word
to each category in the chart on this page. Think of
something that represents the new describing word.

Harcourt

Name _____

▶ **Cut out the clue cards and the word cards. Put a word where it best finishes each sentence clue. Paste a word on each side of the clue cards.**

With five cents, I will [buy] gum.

Apples and plums are [fruit].

Toad [smiled] because he was happy.

In my fluffy coat, I am [warm].

The U.S. flag is red, white, and [blue].

Pumpkins are the color [orange].

In the fall, the leaves turn many [colors].

| buy | fruit | smiled | warm | blue | orange | colors |
| buy | colors | smiled | warm | blue | orange | colors |

Harcourt

Pink and
purple are
colors .

I am not
cold. I am
warm .

I did not
frown. I
smiled .

He buys an
apple and an
orange .

Dad's car
is dark
blue .

What would
you like to
buy ?

The quilt
has many
colors
in it.

Harcourt

Name _____

► **Read the story. Circle all the words with <u>ow</u>. Write all of the words on the chart.**

(Owl) liked the barn. His home was up. (Cow) liked the barn. His home was (down.) "(How) are you?" asked (Owl.) "Right (now) I am hungry," said (Cow.) "Let's go to (town.)" So they went off in a (brown) car.

Owl
Cow
down
How
now
town
brown

TRY THIS Number the words to put them in ABC order.

SCHOOL-HOME CONNECTION With your child, write a four-line rhyme about Cow and Owl. Use the words from the chart to make the rhymes.

Harcourt

Name _____

▶ **Use the words from the box to complete the story.**

how	now	town	brown	down

Toad went high up and looked

_____

_____
down _____. He saw green grass

_____

and _____ brown _____ dirt. He went all over

_____   _____

_____ town _____. Toad knows _____ how _____

to stop. But he does not want to land right

_____

_____ now _____. He's having so

much fun!

SCHOOL-HOME CONNECTION Help your child use the words to write a story about a day he or she would like to spend with Toad.

Harcourt

Name _____

▶ **Think about the story. Then fill in the story map.** Responses will vary.

Beginning

The absent-minded toad made a shopping list.

Middle

He went to the market to shop.

Ending

He forgot about buying what he needed and went home.

Harcourt

SCHOOL-HOME CONNECTION Ask your child to tell you about
The Absent-Minded Toad. Ask him or her if they think the title is a good
one, and why or why not.

Welcome Home
Lesson 27   **73**

Name _____

► **Choose the word that best completes each sentence. Write the word.**

price	drive	hike	ride	hide

1. I could _____ride_____ my bike.

2. Where did I _____hide_____ it?

3. I could _____drive_____ the car.

4. What is the _____price_____ for a cab?

5. So, I'll just _____hike_____ to town!

Welcome Home
Lesson 28

SCHOOL-HOME CONNECTION Use the words to write a story together about two toads who are friends.

Harcourt

Name _____

▶ **Read Toad's shopping list. Circle all the words with the same vowel sound as <u>team</u>.**

Shopping List
(green) apples
(three) oranges
one can (pea) soup
(lean) (beef)
ice (cream)
baked (beans)
(tea) bags
(meat) balls
milk

TRY THIS Count the number of words you circled. Write the number on the shopping list.

SCHOOL-HOME CONNECTION Make a three-column chart with your child. Sort the *ee* and *ea* words in the list.

Welcome Home
Lesson 29   **75**

Harcourt

Name _____

▶ **Toad went to a silly market. Follow
the directions.**

1. Color the green beans pink.

2. Color the corn many colors.

3. Color the carrots purple.

4. Color three tomatoes red and two orange.

5. Color the lettuce white.

6. Color the potatoes green.

SCHOOL-HOME CONNECTION Have your child give
you directions for a simple task. Discuss the directions
you received.

Harcourt

Name _____

▶ **Finish each ad by writing the word that best completes each sentence.**

| place | Lace | face | price |

_____

Lace

your shoes with neat colors.

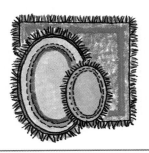

See your

_____

face

here!

No one beats our

_____

price   for

rugs!

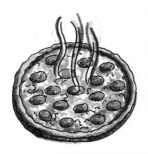

Mama's is the best

_____

place   for

pizza!

SCHOOL-HOME CONNECTION Ask your child to read each word in the box. Say each word and ask him or her to spell it aloud.

Welcome Home
Lesson 30

77

Name _____

► **Read the story. Write the word that best completes the sentence.**

sky	cry	fly	Why	try	tie

1. " _____ Why _____ do you _____ cry _____ ?"

Toad asked.

2. "Because I can't _____ fly _____ to my nest," said Owl.

3. "I need to get up in the _____ sky _____ , but I can't

get my _____ tie _____ out."

4. "I will _____ try _____ to help,"

said Toad.

SCHOOL-HOME CONNECTION Use the words
to write a four-line rhyme about the story.

Harcourt

Name _____

▶ **Read the sentences. Each sentence tells how many. Circle the word that tells how many. Then color how many Frog bought.**

1. Frog got (three) lamps.

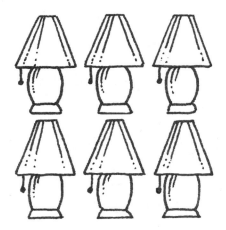

2. Frog picked (five) umbrellas.

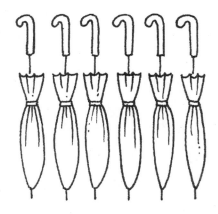

3. He got (two) plants.

4. He got (one) tent.

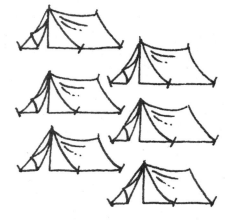

Harcourt

SCHOOL-HOME CONNECTION Ask your child how many plants and lamps Frog bought altogether. Help him or her write an addition sentence that tells how many.

Welcome Home
Lesson 31

79

Name _____

▶ **Read the story. Write the word that best finishes each sentence.**

great	took	heads	might	water

My Camping Trip

Mom and I went camping. We _____ took _____

sleeping bags and a tent. We put the boat in the

_____ water _____. We found a _____ great _____ place to

put the tent. With hats on our _____ heads _____, we went

for a hike. "We _____ might _____ go fishing," said Mom.

Harcourt

Name _____

| cook | food | great | fire |

Later we made a _____fire_____ to _____cook_____ the

soup. We were hungry. We ate all the _____food_____.

We slept in the tent. It was a _____great_____ camping trip!

 TRY THIS Write all the words that have five letters. Write a new story with these words.

SCHOOL-HOME CONNECTION Play a game. Write each vocabulary word on a small card. Mix the cards, and pick two. Say a sentence using both of the words.

Welcome Home
Lesson 32

81

Harcourt

▶ **Write the word in the box that best completes each sentence.**

| pie | cry | by | lie | try |

1. Toad and Owl sit _____ **by** _____ the fire.

2. "Let's eat some _____ **pie** _____," said Toad.

3. Owl starts to _____ **cry** _____.

4. "I can't tell a _____ **lie** _____," said Owl.

   "I ate the pie!"

5. "Don't cry! I'll _____ **try** _____

   to cook some soup.

SCHOOL-HOME CONNECTION Work with your child to write three sentences using the word *by*.

Harcourt

Name _____

▶ **Read the story and circle all the spelling words.**

I can not jump over the moon.
I can not get up in the (sky.) (My)
little dog does not laugh. (My) cat
does not play a song. (My) friends
know cows do not (fly.) They do not
wonder (why.) But they do ask me
how I make the best apple (pie.)

pie   my
why   sky
fly

▶ **Write the spelling words in ABC order.**

1. _____ fly _____

2. _____ my _____

3. _____ pie _____

4. _____ sky _____

5. _____ why _____

Harcourt

SCHOOL-HOME CONNECTION Ask your child to write
some words that end with *y* and *ie*. Together, write a story
with the words.

Name _____

▶ **Think about the story. Then complete the story chart.** Responses will vary.

What does Jack want?

Jack wants something to eat.

What does Jack do?

Jack begins making tumbleweed stew.

Then what happens?

Lots of animals bring vegetables to put in the stew.

How does the story end?

The stew has many vegetables, and all the animals eat until they are full.

SCHOOL-HOME CONNECTION Ask your child to tell you about *Tumbleweed Stew*. Discuss the ending. Brainstorm ideas for Jack Rabbit's cactus pie.

Harcourt

Name _____

▶ **Use the words in the box to complete each asking or telling sentence.**

| Where | Why | Who | When | What | while |

1. _____Who_____ is hungry?

2. _____What_____ is there to eat?

3. _____When_____ will Mother come?

4. _____Why_____ can't we eat now?

5. _____Where_____ is Mother?

6. "We were hungry _____while_____ you were away!"

SCHOOL-HOME CONNECTION Write each asking word on a
small card. Take turns picking one card and using the word to
ask a question.

Welcome Home
Lesson 33   85

Harcourt

Name _____

▶ **Read about armadillos. Then write a sentence to answer each question.**

Armadillos are animals with very hard skin. They are the size of a cat. They have short legs, but they move fast. They eat worms, bugs, and snails. They roll up in a hard ball to keep safe.

1. How big are armadillos?

_____

They are the size of a cat.

2. What is their skin like?

_____

They have hard skin.

3. How do they keep safe?

_____

They roll up in a hard ball.

SCHOOL-HOME CONNECTION Talk or read about an unusual animal with your child. Draw a detailed picture together.

Harcourt

Name _____

► **Look at the picture. Do what the sentences say.**

Another owl is added beside owl. One cactus is green.

Mice are brown.   Snake is red and blue.

1. Color the snake red and blue.

2. Draw another owl next to this one.

3. Color the mice brown.

4. Color a plant green.

Harcourt

SCHOOL-HOME CONNECTION Give your child a
piece of paper and a crayon. Give him or her
simple directions to create a simple drawing.

Welcome Home
Lesson 34   87

Name _____

▶ **Use a contraction to complete each sentence.**

don't	can't	doesn't	Jack's	He's	He'll

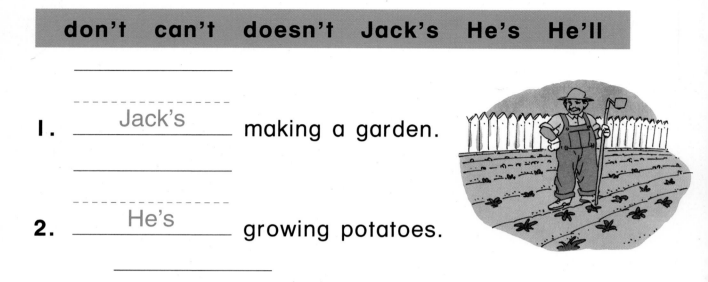

1. _____ Jack's _____ making a garden.

2. _____ He's _____ growing potatoes.

3. He _____ doesn't _____ want animals to eat the plants.

4. _____ He'll _____ make a gate so they _____ can't _____ get in.

5. The animals _____ don't _____ like it!

SCHOOL-HOME CONNECTION Review the contractions. Talk about the two words that make up each contraction.

Harcourt

Name _____

▶ **Write the word that best completes each sentence in the story.**

| home | nose | hole | stove | bone | mole |

1. This is a _____ hole _____ in the dirt.

2. It is the door to my _____ home _____.

3. You see, I am a _____ mole _____.

4. I sniff with my _____ nose _____.

5. I have a _____ stove _____.

6. I will make soup with this _____ bone _____.

SCHOOL-HOME CONNECTION Use the phonograms *-ole* and
-one to form more words with long vowel *o*.

Welcome Home
Lesson 36

89

Harcourt

Name _____

▶ **Read the chart. Then write the word
that best finishes each sentence.**

sunny	**rainy**	**snowy**	**stormy**	**cloudy**

1. It is a _____ sunny _____ day.

2. It is a _____ rainy _____ day.

3. It is a _____ snowy _____ day.

4.  It is a _____ stormy _____ day.

 TRY THIS
Write a story about today's weather.

SCHOOL-HOME CONNECTION Together, read the weather
report in a newspaper. Help your child find words that
describe the weather.

Harcourt

Name _____

▶ **Cut out the word cards. Read the clues in the boxes. Paste each word card below the matching clue.**

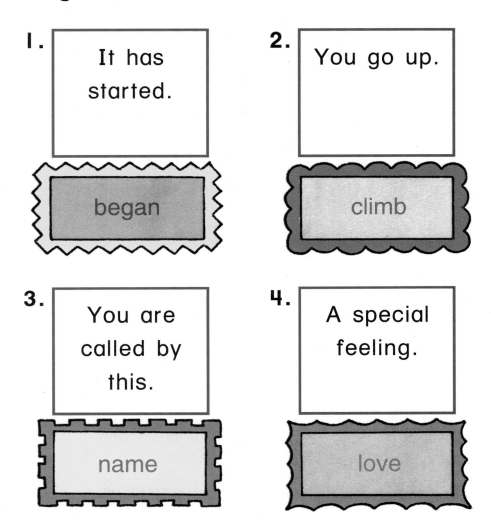

1. It has started.

began

2. You go up.

climb

3. You are called by this.

name

4. A special feeling.

love

| began | climb | love | name |
| began | climb | love | name |

SCHOOL-HOME CONNECTION Three of the vocabulary words contain long vowels. (*began, climb, name*) Help your child listen for the long vowel sounds as you read the words together.

Welcome Home
Lesson 37

91

Harcourt

Name _____

▶ **Use the word cards to finish each sentence. Paste the word card.**

5. My  is Carl.

6. I  up the steps.

7. It 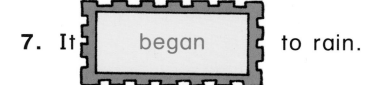 to rain.

8. I would  to go outside.

Welcome Home
Lesson 37

Harcourt

▶ **Read the sentences about Little Bear.**
Write the word that best completes each sentence.

| alone | nose | those | home | close |

1. Little Bear has a little black __nose__.

2. From the top of the tree he saw his __home__.

3. He can't fly like __those__ birds.

4. The little girl was lost and __alone__.

5. I think they will be __close__ friends.

TRY THIS

Use this letter pattern: [ ] [o] [ ] [e]

Write four new words that fit the pattern.

Harcourt

 SCHOOL-HOME CONNECTION Take turns with your child using each word in a new sentence.

Welcome Home
Lesson 37

93

Name _____

▶ **Write the word in the box that best matches the clue.**

bone	home	joke	nose	note

1. It lets us smell things. _____ nose _____

2. We laugh when we hear a silly one. _____ joke _____

3. We do not eat this part, but dogs like it.

_____ bone _____

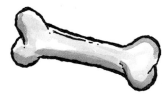

4. This is where you and your family live.

_____ home _____

5. You can read and write one. _____ note _____

TRY THIS Read the spelling words. Where do you hear the vowel sound? Color the box. | beginning | middle | end |

SCHOOL-HOME CONNECTION Write the words in one column. Have your child color in the *o*'s red, and trace the *e*'s in red. Talk about the pattern.

Harcourt

Name _____

▶ **Draw and write about what happens in the beginning, the middle, and the end of the story.** Responses will vary.

Beginning

In the beginning Little Bear climbs the tree and sees many things.

Middle

In the middle Little Bear meets Emily and helps her find her way home.

Ending

At the end Little Bear tells Mother about what he saw, what he did, and that he met a new friend.

SCHOOL-HOME CONNECTION Have your child read his or her sentences to you. Ask your child to tell you what could happen in the next chapter.

Welcome Home
Lesson 37　　95

Name _____

▶ **Read the story. Circle all the words with the same vowel sound as <u>cone</u>.**

Bear (rode) to see his friend (Mole,) but (Mole) was not (home.) Bear left a (note) for (Mole.) "Go to the flag (pole) at the park. We can jump (rope)." Bear (rode) to the park. There was (Mole) and some other friends too!

▶ **Write the words you circled.**

_____

rode, Mole, home, note, pole, rope

_____

_____

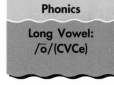

SCHOOL-HOME CONNECTION Use the list of long *o* words to write a new story. Use Raccoon and Skunk in the story.

Harcourt

► **Read about a bear. Circle the word that best completes each sentence. Write the word.**

The White Bear

This bear lives on ice and snow. He is white but has a black nose. When he hides his nose, he is all white. It is hard to spot him on the snow. He hunts birds, rabbits, and seals. He is the biggest of all bears.

white
blue
(**black**)

1. This bear is white but has
_____
a _____ black _____ nose.

(**rabbits**)
bears
plants

2. He hunts _____ rabbits _____ .

sea
beach
(**snow**)

3. He is hard to see in the _____ snow _____ .

oldest
(**biggest**)
smallest

4. He is the _____ biggest _____ of all.

SCHOOL-HOME CONNECTION Talk with your child about pets. Ask him/her to draw a picture of your pet or a friend's pet. Revisit the picture and together add details.

Welcome Home
Lesson 38

97

Harcourt

Name _____

▶ **Tess and Dan are at the ABC Zoo. The animals are in ABC order at this zoo. Write the names of the animals Tess and Dan see as they walk through the ABC Zoo.**

| kangaroo | cheetah | hippo |
| tiger | ostrich | duck |

1. _____cheetah_____

2. _____duck_____

3. _____hippo_____   4. _____kangaroo_____

5. _____ostrich_____

Come Again Soon

6. _____tiger_____

SCHOOL-HOME CONNECTION Cut out 10 small cards. Make one card for each of the six animals at the ABC Zoo. Make four new cards: *ant, worm, pelican, rabbit.* Mix the cards and play a game. Pick one card and begin an ABC list. Take turns picking a card and adding it in the right ABC place.

Name _____

▶ **Add -ed or -ing to the word to complete each sentence. Remember to double the last letter before adding the ending.**

hop + ing

_____

1. Rabbit was _____ hopping _____ through the grass.

stop + ed

_____

2. She _____ stopped _____ to pick flowers.

skip + ing

_____

3. She began _____ skipping _____ home.

hug + ed

_____

4. Mother _____ hugged _____ her.

TRY THIS Make a list of each word with the -ed and the -ing ending. Write a new story using some of these words. Circle the words in your story.

SCHOOL-HOME CONNECTION Ask your child to write the words *clap, wag, mop,* and *hum* on paper. Then write each word with the -ed and -ing endings.

Harcourt

Name _____

▶ **Use the words in the box to complete the sentences. Then read the story again.**

| those | woke | nose | rose | poke |

1. "Did you _____poke_____ me?" asked Father.

2. "I did," said Bear, "with my little black

   _____nose_____."

3. "You _____woke_____ me up."

4. Bear gave Father a _____rose_____.

5. "I was just dreaming about _____those_____!"

6. "My _____nose_____ knows!"

SCHOOL-HOME CONNECTION Make a list of the words in the box. Ask your child to sort them into two lists (-oke, -ose). Add two new words to each list.

Harcourt

Patch's Treat

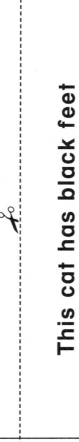

This cat has black feet that look like socks.

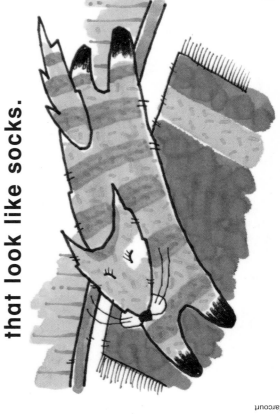

--- Fold ---

--- Fold ---

Patch! Let's go home. You need a treat. I'll feed you.

8

Please, can I keep him? I'll try to keep my room neat.

9

This sweet cat has
a patch on his eye.

Jean needs to find good
homes for her cats.

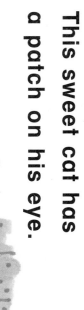

— Fold —

— Fold —

Please, can I keep him?
He'll sleep in a small
bed in my room.

5

What should we call him?

7

Baseball!

1

— Fold —

3

Children in many
countries play the game.
They play in the same way—

6 with a ball, a bat, and a mitt.

— Fold —

People like
to watch the
players step
up to the plate
and hit the ball.
CRACK!

8

2

Baseball is played all over the world. It doesn't take much to play the game. You need a ball, a bat, some mitts, and a big place to play.

4

The game was first played in the United States of America. It was first called "town ball." Later it became baseball.

5

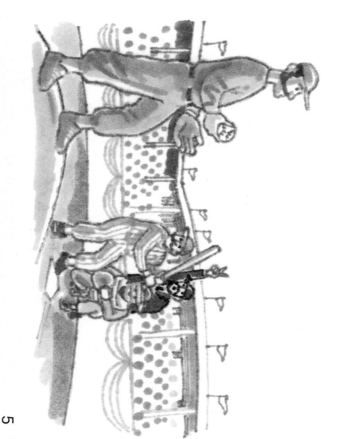

7

Fold

Fold

A Piece of Cake

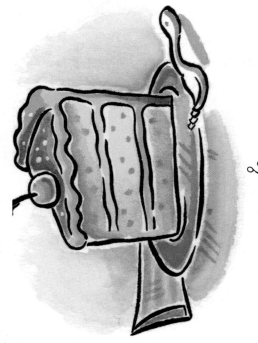

Fold

Oh, yes, that would be nice.
Do you have Sticky Cake?

Fold

This is just like the Silly Cake
8 my Mommy makes!

Aaah! I thought of a cake you
6 must try. We baked it this morning.

2

Would you like a piece
of cake with your tea?

Fold

7

Here is a piece of Silly Cake.
Please tell me how you like it.

Too bad. Do you have
Happy Cake? Or even
Hungry Cake?

5

4

Sticky Cake?
No, we do not have Sticky Cake.

Fold

Once in a While

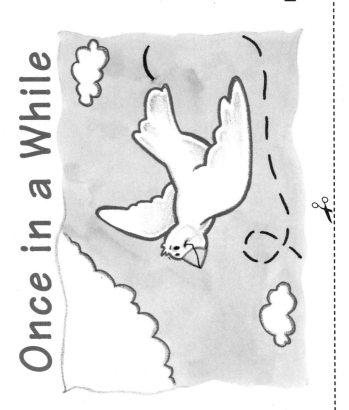

— Fold —

The one with the wide smile
wondered and watched.

Once in a while, four white birds
smile when they wonder about

8 the one with the wide smile.

— Fold —

3

6

2

Five white birds shared the same nest. They ate together. They slept together.

Once in a while, the one with the wide smile talked about going away.

4

One day, the bird with the wide smile went on his way.

7

Once in a while, the others laughed and said he was kidding. 5

How to Make a Face

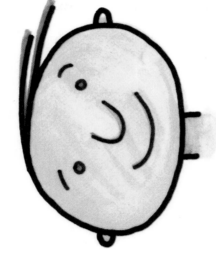

— Fold —

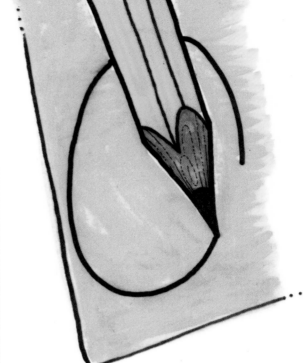

Make a nice big circle.

3

— Fold —

Now you make a pretty face
   yourself.

8

You're almost finished. Make it
look pretty. You can make your
face fancy or simple.

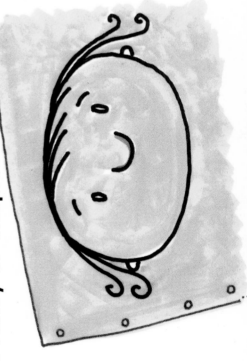

6

4

In the center, make a nose.

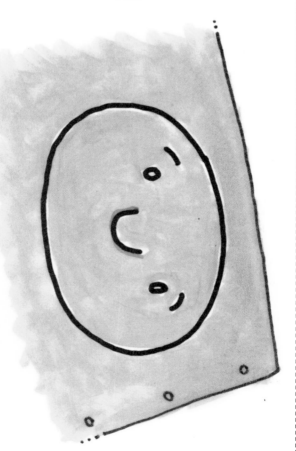

— Fold —

2

First use a pencil.

— Fold —

Don't forget the eyes.

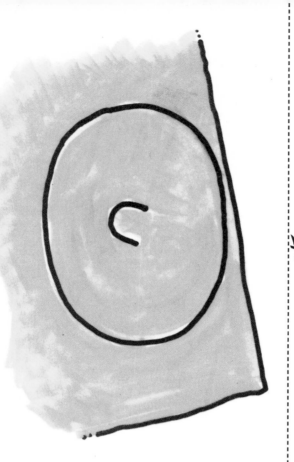

5

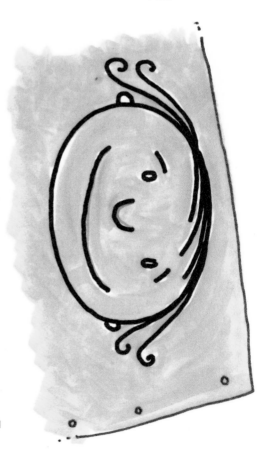

7

Brown Bear's Lunch

— Fold —

Bread
Peanut
Butter
Milk

— Fold —

Brown Bear went back to town.

He got the things on his list

8 and flowers for his friend.

They talked and walked until

Brown Bear was home again.

He forgot about his list, but

6 he didn't forget about his lunch!

WELCOME TO
BEAR TOWN

Welcome Home
Cut-out Fold-up Book

111

2

Brown Bear made a
list of things to buy.

Fold

4

He went to town and met a friend.
"How are you?" he asked. Brown
Bear and his friend talked and
walked and talked.

Fold

5

7

A Dream to Fly

1

Fold

"Some day I'll go up in the sky. I want to try."

3

Fold

I LOVE TO FLY

If you look in the sky, you might see Mike way up high.

8

Well, Mike got his wish. He got in a plane.

9

4

Mike went to school.
He wasn't shy.

2

Mike had a dream.
He wanted to fly.

— Fold —

— Fold —

"I'm going to fly. It's my
dream to go up in the sky."

5

"It's as easy as pie!
Look, I can fly!"

7

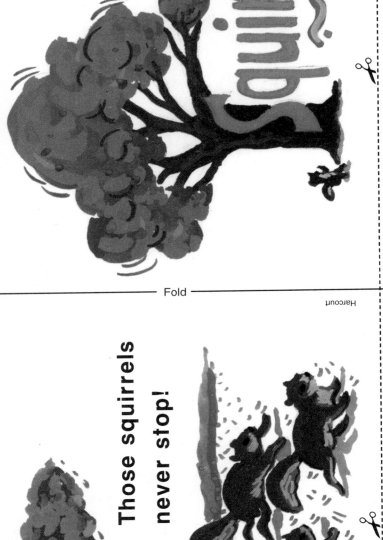

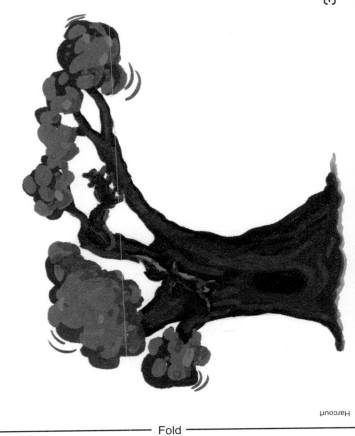

1

3

Fold

Fold

Those squirrels never stop!

8

Red, brown, and black squirrels quickly climb up trees and poles. Have you ever seen a squirrel hop from branch to branch?

6

Squirrels can be found
all over the world.
Some squirrels
build homes
in trees.

2

4

Squirrels like to
dig holes for their
winter food. Their
sharp teeth help
them crack open
nuts and seeds.

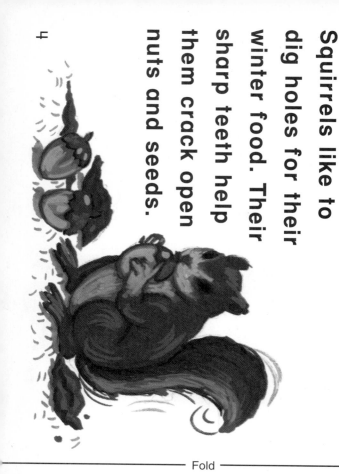

5

7

Fold

Fold

Set
Sail

▶ **Say each word. Circle the pictures that have the same vowel sound as <u>sight</u>. Then write the word.**

high	fright	night	sigh	light

1.

_____

- - - - - - - - - -

_____

2.

_____

- - - - - - - - - -

light

3.

_____

- - - - - - - - - -

night

4.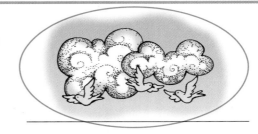

_____

- - - - - - - - - -

high

5.

_____

- - - - - - - - - -

fright

6.

_____

- - - - - - - - - -

_____

SCHOOL-HOME CONNECTION Ask your child to show you the completed page. Let your child explain the answers he or she did not pick.

Harcourt

▶ Add <u>er</u> or <u>est</u> to the word so that it correctly completes the sentence. Write the word on the line.

bright
_____

1. This bird has _____brighter_____

colors than that bird.

_____

high
_____

2. The blue bird lands on a _____higher_____

branch than the green bird.

_____

tight
_____

3. Birds make nests in the _____tightest_____

places.

TRY THIS With a partner, act out the words <u>light</u>, <u>lighter</u>, <u>lightest</u> and <u>high</u>, <u>higher</u>, <u>highest</u>.

SCHOOL-HOME CONNECTION Have your child read you the completed page, and show you how he or she chose the answers.

Set Sail
Lesson 1

3

▶ **Look at the blue bird's pictures. Write
the word that best completes each sentence.**

joined   afraid

_____

1. I was ___afraid___ to fly.

learn   flew

_____

2. I will ___learn___ how
to fly.

afraid   flew

_____

3. Mom ___flew___ away.

afraid   joined

_____

4. A little green bird ___joined___
me for a walk.

Harcourt

joined   afraid

_____

- - - - - - - - - - - - - - - - - - -

5. I was not _____ afraid _____ to fly any more.

flew   afraid

_____

- - - - - - - - - - - - - - - - - - -

6. I _____ flew _____ for a long time.

joined   afraid

_____

- - - - - - - - - - - - - - - - - - -

7. I _____ joined _____ another bird.

learn   flew

_____

- - - - - - - - - - - - - - - - - - -

8. I think it is fun to _____ learn _____ how to fly.

TRY THIS Make a drawing that shows how to help someone try a new thing. Write a sentence to go with the picture.

SCHOOL-HOME CONNECTION Read the completed page with your child. Write or say two rhyming sentences with the words *flew* and *grew*.

Set Sail
Lesson 2

5

Harcourt

Name _____

▶ **Circle the words that have the same vowel sound as <u>might</u>.**

1. branch 	**2.** (light) 
3. (night) 	**4.** (high) 
5. (fright) 	**6.** nest 

 TRY THIS Write another word that rhymes with <u>sight</u>. Draw a picture for it.

SCHOOL-HOME CONNECTION Ask your child to show you the completed page. Let them explain the words he or she did *not* pick.

Harcourt

Name _____

▶ **Write the word that best completes each sentence.**

| might | high | light | night | right |

_____

1. Birds fly _____ high _____ in the sky.

2. Do birds fly by day or

   at _____ night _____ ?

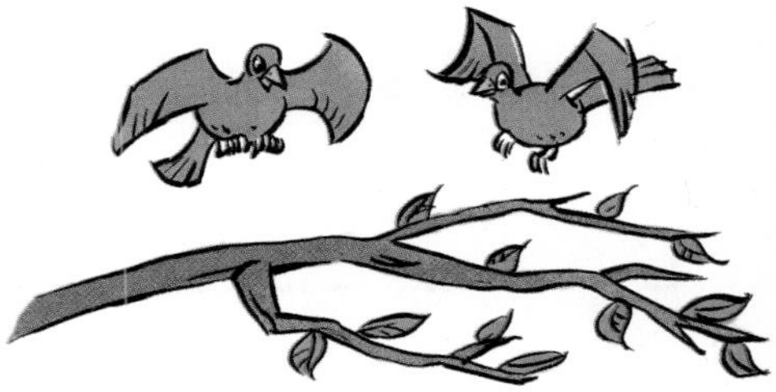

3. A bird _____ might _____ make its nest in a tree.

4. One nest is _____ right _____ here in this tree.

5. The eggs get heat and _____ light _____ from the sun.

Set Sail
Lesson 2   **7**

Name _____

▶ **Think about the story. Then complete
the flowchart.**

The blue bird is afraid to fly.

The blue bird asks his mother what is out there.

He looks for nothing.

All the birds look for nothing.

The blue bird comes home.

Write a new ending for the story you read.

SCHOOL-HOME CONNECTION Think of a story you both
know. Retell it to each other.

Harcourt

▶ **Read the paragraph. Write the main idea in the box. Write the details in the circles.**

Ducks are born knowing many things. Ducklings know that they must follow their mother. Ducklings also know how to swim. The mother does not have to show them. Answers may vary.

Main Idea

Ducks are born knowing many things.

Mother does not have to show them.

Ducklings also know how to swim.

Ducklings know that they must follow their mother.

TRY THIS Think of a pet or other animal you know. Find out what things that animal knows when it is born. Find out what things the animal has to learn.

SCHOOL-HOME CONNECTION Ask your child to read the paragraph at the top of this page to you. Together, think of a title for the paragraph.

Set Sail
Lesson 3

9

Harcourt

▶ **Read the story. Then choose the best answer. Fill in the oval in front of the best answer.**

Bird Baths

Help a bird have a bath. Put a plastic pan outside. A table is a good spot. Put in a little water. Don't make it too deep. The birds will love it.

1. What is this story about?
   - ⬤ how you can make a birdbath
   - ⬯ how much water to put in a birdbath
   - ⬯ why you should use a plastic pan

2. What sentence tells you the main idea?
   - ⬯ The birds will love it.
   - ⬤ Help a bird have a bath.
   - ⬯ Put in a little water.

3. Which sentence tells a detail about the story?
   - ⬯ The birds will love it.
   - ⬯ Help a bird have a bath.
   - ⬤ Put in a little water.

SCHOOL-HOME CONNECTION Tell your child that this page is to help them learn how to fill out a special kind of answer form that they will use at times while they are in school.

Harcourt

Name _____

▶ **Choose the word that completes the sentence. Write it on the line.**

perch   port   porch
_____

1. A large bird landed on my _____ *porch* _____ .

corn   cork   cake
_____

2. I gave it some _____ *corn* _____ to eat.

shirt   short   sport
_____

3. It stayed only a _____ *short* _____ time.

storm   torn   stork
_____

4. It was a _____ *stork* _____ .

short   sort   porch
_____

5. I have never seen that _____ *sort* _____ of bird.

SCHOOL-HOME CONNECTION Have your child find the word *stork* on the page.

Set Sail
Lesson 4   **11**

Harcourt

Name _____

▶ **Read each sentence. Write the word that completes the sentence. Remember to drop the <u>e</u>.**

surprise + ed
_____

1. The bird was _____ surprised _____.

taste + ed
_____

2. She _____ tasted _____ blueberries.

chase + ing
_____

3. "No one is _____ chasing _____ me," she said.

believe + ed
_____

4. "I never _____ believed _____ I could fly."

TRY THIS Add <u>-ed</u> or <u>-ing</u> to the words <u>taste</u>, <u>like</u>, and <u>bake</u>. Write a sentence for each new word.

SCHOOL-HOME CONNECTION Ask your child to read you the completed page. Add -ing to answer words that end with -ed, and make new sentences with those words.

Name _____

▶ **Circle the word that names the picture. Then write the word.**

1.

hat   hot   (hay)

_____

- - - - - - - - - - - - - -
hay
_____

2.

pan   play   (paint)

_____

- - - - - - - - - - - - - -
paint
_____

3.

(rain)   ride   rail

_____

- - - - - - - - - - - - - -
rain
_____

4.

snack   sail   (snail)

_____

- - - - - - - - - - - - - -
snail
_____

5.

(tray)   tail   trap

_____

- - - - - - - - - - - - - -
tray
_____

6.

tree   tired   (train)

_____

- - - - - - - - - - - - - -
train
_____

TRY THIS Write a word that rhymes with <u>hay</u> and has <u>ay</u>. Write a word that rhymes with <u>snail</u> and has <u>ai</u>. Draw a picture for each word.

SCHOOL-HOME CONNECTION Ask your child to share the finished page with you. Together, make up a sentence for each answer.

Set Sail
Lesson 6   13

Harcourt

Name _____

▶ **Look at the picture. Write a verb to complete each sentence.**

| play | stay | wait | mail |

_____

1. Frog wanted Toad to __play__ ball.

_____

2. Toad wanted to __mail__ a letter first.

_____

3. Frog said, "I will sit and __wait__ for you."

_____

4. Toad asked Frog to __stay__ for supper.

TRY THIS Work with a partner. Make a list of as many verbs as you can.

 SCHOOL-HOME CONNECTION With your child, look for some other verbs on this page. (*asked, said, sit, wanted*)

Harcourt

Name _____

▶ **Cut out the cards and play a matching
game. Match each word with the sentence
it completes.**

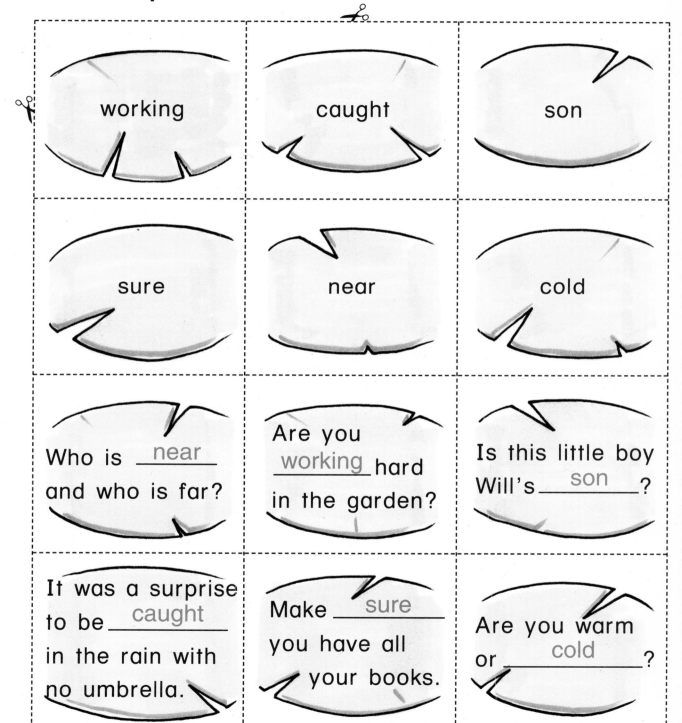

working

caught

son

sure

near

cold

Who is ___near___ and who is far?

Are you ___working___ hard in the garden?

Is this little boy Will's ___son___?

It was a surprise to be ___caught___ in the rain with no umbrella.

Make ___sure___ you have all your books.

Are you warm or ___cold___?

Harcourt

🚚 **SCHOOL-HOME CONNECTION** Work with your child to create
sentences that include the vocabulary words.

Name _____

Harcourt

Name _____

▶ **Look at the picture. Then write the word from the box that completes each sentence.**

play	stay	day	rain	wait

1. I do not like the _____rain_____.

2. I can't _____play_____ outside.

3. I don't want to _____stay_____ home.

4. I want a sunny _____day_____.

5. I will _____wait_____

for the sun to come out.

 TRY THIS Use the words <u>mail</u>, <u>day</u>, and <u>gray</u> to write a short poem or story about the weather.

 SCHOOL-HOME CONNECTION Ask your child to read you the completed page. Together, make up a few sentences about what the toad did after the sun came out. Use words with *ai* and *ay*.

Harcourt

Name _____

▶ **Write the word that best completes each**
sentence. Circle the <u>ay</u> or <u>ai</u> in the words
that you write.

| day | rain | may | tail | play |

1. Ray, can you come out and _____ play _____ ?

2. It is a sunny, warm spring _____ day _____ .

3. What did you say? You _____ may _____ ?

4. Do you think it will _____ rain _____ ?

5. The puppy chases after

its _____ tail _____ .

SCHOOL-HOME CONNECTION Have your child
show you the different ways long *a* is spelled.

Harcourt

Name _____

► **Frog hears that spring is just around the corner. Color the blocks that tell where Frog goes in the story.**

kissed his mother	walked down a path	
walked into a cave	walked in the meadow	
walked on big stones	walked along the river	walked in a field of corn
swam at the beach	went around his house	jumped in the lake

► **How do you know when it is spring?**

Responses will vary.

SCHOOL-HOME CONNECTION Discuss with your child how the phrase "spring is just around the corner" means spring is coming soon.

Harcourt

Name _____

▶ **Read the story to find out where the snail went. Draw his trail. Then circle all of the words that have the same vowel sound as <u>may</u>.**

(Snail's) (Rainy) (Day)

(Rainy) (days) made (Snail) happy. He (played) on the steps, and then he (came) down. (Snail) (played) in the (pail), but liked (playing) with (paint) the most. He (played) on the (drain). He (played) under the (mailbox). At the (bay), (Snail) saw a ship with a (sail). He got on and (sailed) (away).

TRY THIS Use the words <u>sail</u>, <u>train</u>, and <u>main</u> to tell more about what the snail did after he got on the ship.

SCHOOL-HOME CONNECTION Read the story aloud. Have your child clap each time you read a word with long vowel *a*.

Harcourt

▶ **Read the word above each line. Add -ed or -ing to the word to complete the sentence. Remember to drop the e.**

like
_____

1. I have always _____ liked _____ spring.

rake
_____

2. My dad is _____ raking _____ the leaves.

chase
_____

3. I do not like _____ chasing _____ snowflakes.

make
_____

4. Are you _____ making _____ a snowman?

bake
_____

5. We _____ baked _____ cookies.

SCHOOL-HOME CONNECTION Read the completed page with your child. Discuss your favorite seasons. Use words with -ed and -ing.

Set Sail
Lesson 10   **21**

Name _____

▶ **Choose the words that best complete the sentence. Write the words on the lines.**

mail **main**	**1.** What is the _____ *main* _____ thing you like about _____ *mail* ?
pail **pain**	**2.** Jake was in _____ *pain* when he tripped over the _____ *pail* .
trail **train**	**3.** The _____ *train* went past an old forest _____ *trail* .

TRY THIS List as many words as you can that rhyme with <u>main</u> or <u>mail</u>. Give yourself one minute.

SCHOOL-HOME CONNECTION Ask your child to show you the completed page. If necessary, help him or her complete the page.

Harcourt

Name _____

▶ **Choose a word in the box that rhymes with each underlined word and makes sense. Write it on the line.**

find	behind	wild

1. Do you <u>mind</u>? There's a large

_____

frog _____behind_____ us.

2. At the zoo, a <u>child</u> read a sign. It said,

_____

"Do not feed our _____wild_____ animals."

3. You need to <u>wind</u> this toy.

_____

The baby will _____find_____

it and play with it.

 TRY THIS Make your own pair of sentences with two words from the box or other words that rhyme with them.

Harcourt

SCHOOL-HOME CONNECTION Discuss the finished page with your child. Help him or her notice the *i* sound in each word.

Set Sail
Lesson 11   **23**

▶ **Write the verb that best completes each sentence.**

drink	find	help	make	fill

1. I ___fill___ the birdbath.

2. Birds ___drink___ from it.

3. They come and ___find___ seeds in our feeder.

4. We ___help___ birds because we like them.

5. I ___make___ bird feeders for my friends.

TRY THIS Work with a friend to read a news story about a sports team. Together, find the verbs that tell about now.

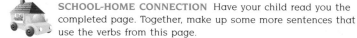

Harcourt

Name _____

▶ **Read each sentence. Cut out the words at the bottom of the page. Paste the words in the correct place to finish each sentence.**

1. I like to [listen] to the rain.

2. Do you [care] for puddles?

3. Of [course] I do.

4. Rainy days are [different] .

5. What was the [largest] puddle you ever saw?

6. You [told] me about that.

✂

| listen | told | different |
| care | largest | course |

SCHOOL-HOME CONNECTION Check that your child has pasted the words in the correct place. Review the vocabulary words and their meanings.

Set Sail
Lesson 12   25

Harcourt

Name _____

Set Sail
Lesson 12

Harcourt

Name _____

▶ **Choose the word from the box to best complete each sentence.**

| find | behind | wild | blind | mind |

1. It can see.

_____

It is not _____ blind _____ .

2. It is not tame.

_____

It is _____ wild _____ .

3. It is not lost.

_____

I can _____ find _____ it .

4. A tadpole's tail is not in front.

_____

It is _____ behind _____ .

5. A tadpole doesn't think like we do.

_____

It has a _____ mind _____ of its own .

SCHOOL-HOME CONNECTION Ask your child to show you the finished page. Together use the sentences to make up a definition for each word in the box.

Harcourt

Name _____

► **Circle the words in the puzzle. Then use them to answer the questions.**

| child | kind | wild | find | mild |

```
s   o   w   i   l   d   k   n   d
s   i   n   g   c   h   i   l   d
m   i   l   d   n   a   n   e   s
a   c   x   f   i   n   d   o   p
```

1. This _____ child _____ plays in the rain.

2. It is a soft, _____ mild _____ rain.

3. He jumps like a _____ wild _____ animal.

4. What _____ kind _____ of animal is he?

5. I will _____ find _____ out!

SCHOOL-HOME CONNECTION Ask your child to tell you how the words *child*, *wild*, and *mild* are the same, and how they are different.

Harcourt

Name _____

▶ **Think about the story. Then fill in the story map.** Answers may vary.

1. What does the
boy's mother say?

He has to stay out of
the puddles, but he can
sail his boat in them.

2. What is the boy's
first problem?

A frog takes his boat
away.

3. How is this problem
solved?

An alligator gets the
boat for him.

4. What problem does
the boy face next?

A pig jumps into the
puddle and splashes the
boy.

5. How does the
elephant solve this
problem?

The elephant drinks up
all the water and then
splashes the animals.

6. What happens at the
end of the story?

The sun comes out, and
the boy goes home and
has a bath.

TRY THIS Circle the parts of the story map that you think could
really happen.

SCHOOL-HOME CONNECTION Read this page
together with your child. Discuss problems and
solutions in daily activities.

Harcourt

Name _____

▶ **Read each sentence. Write <u>real</u> or <u>not real</u> on the lines.**

1. He can sail a boat. _____ real

2. The cat can sail a boat. _____ not real

3. Fish need raincoats. _____ not real

4. Rain makes puddles. _____ real

5. He can think about a cat. _____ real

TRY THIS Pick one of the sentences that tells about something not real. Draw a picture of it. Write <u>not real</u> under it.

SCHOOL-HOME CONNECTION Have your child share the completed page. Together, list some other things that are *real* or *not real*.

Harcourt

Name _____

▶ **Write the word from the box that best completes each sentence.**

large	age	bridge	edge

1. I came to a _____large_____ puddle.

2. An alligator sat by the

_____edge_____ of the puddle.

3. I wanted a _____bridge_____ so

I could get over the puddle.

4. Kids my _____age_____ like puddles.

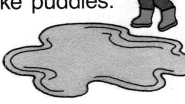

Harcourt

TRY THIS Make a chart about the ages of your classmates. Give your chart a title that uses the word <u>age</u>.

SCHOOL-HOME CONNECTION Ask your child to read you the finished page. Together, think of as many words as you can that have the soft *g* sound.

Set Sail
Lesson 14   31

Name _____

▶ **Look at the picture. Write the word to complete the sentence. Remember to double the last letter before you add ed or ing.**

step + ed
_____

1. Marco _____ stepped _____ outside.

slip + ing
_____

2. He began _____ slipping _____ and fell!

stop + ed
_____

3. Marco _____ stopped _____ to think.

snap + ed
_____

4. He _____ snapped _____ his fingers and went back inside.

step + ing
_____

5. Marco is _____ stepping _____ into his skates.

Harcourt

SCHOOL-HOME CONNECTION Ask your child to show you the completed page. Work together to write new sentences for the answer words.

Name _____

▶ **Read the numbered clues. Use the words from the box to complete the puzzle.**

hello	gold	no	also
ago	cold	soda	go

Across

2. a long time ___

3. ____ pop

4. stop and __

6. _____, how are you?

Down

1. icy ____

2. me ____ (too)

4. silver and ____

5. __, thanks

(Crossword puzzle)

1. (down) c
2. (across) a g o — (down) a l l — 3. (across) s o d a
4. (across) g o — (down) o, d — 5. (down) n
6. (across) h e l l o

SCHOOL-HOME CONNECTION Ask your child to share the completed page. Then work together to list some words that rhyme with *old*, and to write some clues for these words. See if a friend can guess the words.

Set Sail
Lesson 16

33

Harcourt

Name _____

▶ **Write <u>am</u>, <u>is</u>, or <u>are</u> to finish each sentence.**

1. What _____<u>are</u>_____ you doing?

2. I _____<u>am</u>_____ playing with a yo-yo.

3. _____<u>Are</u>_____ you good at it?

4. My sister _____<u>is</u>_____ better.

5. She _____<u>is</u>_____ helping me.

6. I _____<u>am</u>_____ taking lessons from her.

TRY THIS Work with a partner to answer the question "What are you doing?" Answer two ways—beginning with "I am" and with "We are."

SCHOOL-HOME CONNECTION Take turns with your child making up new sentences using *am*, *is*, and *are*.

Harcourt

Name _____

▶ **Choose the word that best completes each sentence. Write it on the line.**

boy
buy
but

1. I need to find the ____boy____.

and
air
at

2. Is he up in the ____air____?

both
buy
best

3. I can't see ____both____ near and far.

flew
few
five

4. Do you see a ____few____ boys down the street?

edge
egg
each

5. They are on the ____edge____ of the puddle.

Harcourt

bought   brought
_____

- - - - - - - - - - - - - - - - - - - -
6. I _____ brought _____ my glasses.

edge   eggs
_____

- - - - - - - - - - - - - -
7. It scares me to look over the _____ edge _____.

▶ **Look for the vocabulary words in this puzzle.**

1. | c | a | r | (a | i | r) | c | a | t |
2. | t | h | (b | r | o | u | g | h | t) |
3. | g | o | o | d | (e | d | g | e) | l |
4. | (b | o | t | h) | m | e | m | i | t |
5. | f | i | v | e | (f | e | w) | m | e |

TRY THIS Make a list of the things a squirrel might want to find in a bed.

SCHOOL-HOME CONNECTION With children, review vocabulary words and their meanings.

Harcourt

Name _____

▶ **Choose the word that best completes each sentence. Write it on the line.**

fold   old   told

_____

1. Mr. Rabbit is stuck in his _____*old*_____ bed.

go   so   got

_____

2. Mr. and Mrs. Rabbit _____*go*_____ get a new bed.

soda   spot   sofa

_____

3. Mr. Rabbit sees a nice _____*sofa*_____.

Old   Sold   Socks

_____

4. Mr. and Mrs. Rabbit say, "_____*Sold*_____!"

 TRY THIS Make up some rhyming sentences using the words sold, old, and told. Say your sentences to the class.

SCHOOL–HOME CONNECTION Have your child find the long *o* words that were not used as answers. Ask him or her to read them aloud and explain why they weren't the answers.

Set Sail
Lesson 17   37

Harcourt

Name _____

▶ **Write the word that best completes each sentence.**

both	go	old	no	Oh

1. "_____Oh_____!" said Bear.

2. "My hat is so _____old_____."

3. "You have _____no_____ hat at all."

4. "We must _____go_____ to the hat store."

5. "We _____both_____ will go."

SCHOOL-HOME CONNECTION Look over the answers your child wrote. Ask him or her to circle the letter *o* in each word.

Harcourt

► **Think about how Poppleton shopped for
a new bed. Fill in the web to show what he did.**

Accept reasonable
responses.

lay down

ate crackers

How Poppleton
tested the bed

watched TV

listened to
bluebirds

**TRY
THIS** Think about your favorite place. Make a list of things
you like to do there.

Harcourt

▶ **Circle the sentence that tells about each picture.**

1. ("Let's go!" said the colt.)

   "No!" said the girl.

   "Hello!" said the ant.

2. A pig thinks he is cold.

   (A pig thinks he has lost his gold.)

   A pig thinks he has lost his tie.

3. I am opening the house now.

   I am over on the sofa.

   (I am holding the gold in this safe.)

4. (I have a total of 3 bags.)

   I have a total of 3 cans.

   I have a folded coat.

5. "Have no fear! Cold soda is here!"

   "Have no fear! Your sofa is here!"

   ("Have no fear! Colt and the gold are here!")

6. (The pig holds his gold.)

   The colt keeps the gold.

   The colt calls the pig.

SCHOOL-HOME CONNECTION Review the completed page with your child. Then make up a new adventure for the superhero colt.

Harcourt

▶ **Look at the picture. Then do what the sentences tell you to do.**

1. Make the pig on stage pink.

2. Give the pig a huge hat.

3. Find the largest bed. Put a badge on it.

4. Draw a huge pillow on one edge of the bed.

5. Find the cage next to the largest bed. Draw a pet gerbil inside the cage.

6. A large crowd is watching from the bridge. Draw a ring around the large crowd.

TRY THIS Write a sentence about this picture. Use some of the words from the sentences under the picture.

SCHOOL-HOME CONNECTION Go over the completed page with your child. Then have your child circle the words that contain the /j/ sound.

Set Sail
Lesson 19   41

Harcourt

Name _____

► **Finish each sentence. Write the contraction for the two words above each sentence.**

They've	You've	You'd	We'd	We're

We are

_____

1. ___We're___ in our new bed.

We would

_____

2. ___We'd___ love you to come see.

You have

_____

3. ___You've___ been here before.

They have

_____

4. ___They've___ got their own bed.

TRY THIS Make a list of things you would like. Begin each item on your list with the words I'd like.

SCHOOL-HOME CONNECTION Ask your child to read the completed page aloud to you. Help your child use each contraction in a sentence.

Harcourt

▶ **Add the ending <u>ed</u> and <u>ing</u> to each word. Remember to drop the final <u>e</u>.**

	ed	ing
close	closed	closing
scare	scared	scaring
snore	snored	snoring

▶ **Write the correct word from the chart to finish each sentence.**

1. Why am I _____ closing _____ this door?

2. The pig is _____ snoring _____ in his sleep.

 SCHOOL-HOME CONNECTION Read your child's completed sentences aloud. Have him or her say "stop" each time you get to a word with an *-ed* or an *-ing* ending. If your child has difficulty identifying the ending by hearing it, have him or her point to the word on the page.

Set Sail
Lesson 20   43

► **Circle the word that best completes each sentence. Then write the word.**

1. "The moon is _____ huge _____," said the cat.

hand
(huge)
tube

2. "It smells like _____ perfume _____," said the mule.

(perfume)
cute
perform

3. The cat sniffed but could not smell

the _____ perfume _____.

purple
(perfume)
huge

4. "_____ Excuse _____ me, but it has no smell," said the cat.

Every
(Excuse)
Cube

5. "Oh! _____ Excuse _____ me!" said the mule. "I was sniffing the flowers."

Empty
Plume
(Excuse)

SCHOOL-HOME CONNECTION Ask your child to read the completed page to you. Then ask your child to explain in his or her own words what the story is about.

Harcourt

▶ **Write the word that best completes
each sentence.**

| spilled | filled | needed | cleaned |

1. Luke _____ needed _____ to make ice cubes.

2. He _____ filled _____ the ice tray with water.

3. The water _____ spilled _____ all over.

4. Luke _____ cleaned _____ up
the mess.

 TRY THIS Take turns with a partner reading the sentences and
acting them out.

SCHOOL-HOME CONNECTION Have your child read the completed
page to you. Ask him or her to tell you what the words would be if
they were action words about the present time.

Set Sail
Lesson 21   45

Name _____

▶ **Read each clue and look at the picture. Then write the clue word that best completes each sentence.**

appear	break	clear	idea	quietly

1. Don't yell or shout.

_____

Be sure to talk __quietly__ .

2. This starts inside your mind.

_____

It's an __idea__ .

3. It's not there.

_____

Can you make it __appear__ ?

4. The stars shine bright. The sky

_____

is very __clear__ tonight.

Harcourt

5. Rabbit and Mole were tired.

_____

They took a _____ break _____.

▶ **Look at the letters on the puzzle. Then write each vocabulary word where it fits on the puzzle.**

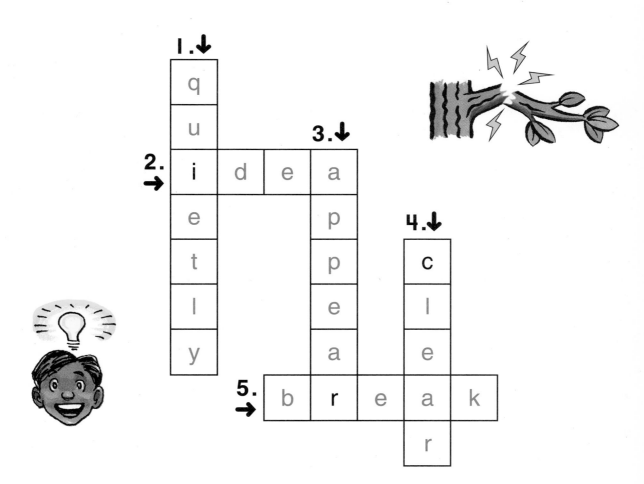

1.↓ q u i d e a
2.→ i d e a
3.↓ a p p e a
4.↓ c l e a
e t l y
5.→ b r e a k
r

TRY THIS Make up your own clues and sentences for each word. See if a partner can answer them.

SCHOOL-HOME CONNECTION Make clues for your child for each of the answer words on the page.

Set Sail
Lesson 22   47

Harcourt

Name _____

▶ **Write the words in the box that will finish the story.**

cube	huge	Excuse	cute

_____

" _____Excuse_____ me," said Mole. "I am never coming

out! I am small, but I want to be _____huge_____.

I want my den to be shaped like a _____cube_____."

"Please come out! You are _____cute_____,"

Mule said. "You are my good friend, too."

SCHOOL-HOME CONNECTION Work with your child to write
original sentences for the words *cute, huge, cube,* and *excuse*.

Harcourt

Name _____

▶ **Write the word in the box that best completes each sentence.**

| cute | use | rude | mule | cube |

1. My _____ mule _____ is on the moon.

2. Is the moon a _____ cube _____?

3. Can you _____ use _____ your ears to hear the moon?

4. Is it _____ rude _____ to stare at the moon?

5. Do you see a _____ cute _____ face in the moon?

SCHOOL-HOME CONNECTION Ask your child which questions have answers that are true and which questions have a false answer. Ask your child to write a true sentence about the moon.

Set Sail
Lesson 22   **49**

Name _____

▶ **Think about the story. Then fill in the story map.** Accept reasonable responses.

Title:
Moon Rope

Characters:
Fox, Mole, Birds

What is the first problem?
When Fox throws the rope, it falls and hits him on the head.

How is it solved?
Mole thinks of having the birds carry the rope to the moon. They do.

What is the second problem?
As Mole and Fox climb to the moon, Mole slips and falls.

How is it solved?
He lands on the back of a bird who carries him to Earth.

What do we learn about Fox and Mole?
Fox can still be seen in the face of the moon. Mole still hides under the ground so no one will laugh at him.

SCHOOL-HOME CONNECTION Ask your child to retell the story of *Moon Rope* with this completed page as a guide.

Harcourt

Name _____

▶ **Circle and write the word that best completes each sentence.**

(**night**)
noise
new

1. It happened late last _____ night _____.

built
(**bright**)
brother

2. The sky was very _____ bright _____.

rolled
(**right**)
ready

3. The birds flew _____ right _____ over us.

should
(**sight**)
shout

4. This _____ sight _____ was a big surprise.

mother
mixed
(**might**)

5. You _____ might _____ see it too.

SCHOOL-HOME CONNECTION With your child, recite the poem that begins "Star light, star bright." Ask your child to identify the words that end in *ight*. Write the words to the poem on paper and have your child circle the *ight* words

Harcourt

▶ **Write the word from the box that best completes each sentence.**

We've	You're	We're	I'd

1. ___We're___ here!

2. ___We've___ been riding so long!

3. ___I'd___ like to take your bags.

4. ___You're___ tired.

Come on in.

 TRY THIS Write a poem about a day at the beach. Use words with '_ve_, '_d_, and '_re_.

SCHOOL-HOME CONNECTION Ask your child to share with you the completed page. Take turns reading the sentences.

► **Circle the word that fits best in each sentence. Write it on the line to complete the sentence.**

(**hoping**)

hoped

host

1. I am _____ *hoping* _____ to get something new.

(**placing**)

placed

place

2. I will be _____ *placing* _____ it in my yard.

Raked

(**Raking**)

Rake

3. _____ *Raking* _____ each fall will not be hard.

tasting

taste

(**tasted**)

4. I have _____ *tasted* _____ the fruit. Try some.

like

(**liked**)

liking

5. I saw it and _____ *liked* _____ it and planted it too.

Harcourt

SCHOOL-HOME CONNECTION Ask your child to read the completed page to you. Have him or her write the base word for *hoping*. (*hope*)

▶ **Read the words in the box and look at the pictures. Then finish each postcard.**

knee	remember	straight

Dear Joey,

 Last night, Dad and I went out. We watched the moon come up. It seemed to come

_____

straight _____ up over the sea.

I found a big pink shell right next to my

_____ knee . I remember _____

that you like shells. When can you come over and see it?

 Your pal,

 Spencer

Harcourt

Dear Spencer,

I was happy to get your card. The moon is full and

_____ remember _____

shiny right now. I am glad you _____

that I like shells. When you get back, I'll come

_____

straight _____ to your house. I want to

see this shell up close. It looks like it is as big

_____

as your _____ knee _____ !

Your best buddy,

Joey

SCHOOL-HOME CONNECTION Have your child choose one of the vocabulary words. Together, think of words that can be formed with the letters in the vocabulary word. Have your child write them and check.

Set Sail
Lesson 26   55

Harcourt

Name _____

▶ **Fill in the story frame to tell about the story. Draw a picture for each sentence.**

Possible responses given.

The Big Big Sea

Beginning
Mama takes the girl out for a walk at night.

Middle
Mama and the girl see the moon and play in the sea.

End
Mama carries the girl back home.

SCHOOL-HOME CONNECTION Review a simple story you and your child know and discuss the beginning, the middle, and the end.

Harcourt

▶ **Write <u>was</u> or <u>were</u> to complete each sentence. Then circle <u>one</u> or <u>more than one</u> to show how many people or things the action word tells about.**

one

1. I _____was_____ skating all day. **more than one**

---

one

2. They _____were_____ skating, too. (**more than one**)

---

one

3. We _____were_____ in a pile! (**more than one**)

---

one

4. We _____were_____ all okay. (**more than one**)

TRY THIS Together with a classmate, tell about three things that happened yesterday. Use <u>was</u> and <u>were</u> in your discussion.

SCHOOL-HOME CONNECTION Ask your child to read this page to you and explain his or her answers.

Set Sail
Lesson 26 **57**

▶ **Write the word that best completes each sentence.**

might	night	flight	light

1. Look at the birds in _____ flight _____.

2. We saw them last _____ night _____, too.

3. I can see by the _____ light _____ of the moon.

4. They _____ might _____ come again.

TRY THIS Write these answer words as a list. Then list all the other words you can with <u>igh</u> that stand for the long <u>i</u> sound.

SCHOOL-HOME CONNECTION With your child, recite the poem that begins, "Star light, star bright." Ask your child to identify the words that end in *ight*. Write the words to the poem on paper so that your child can see as well as hear the *ight* words.

Harcourt

Name _____

► **Write the word from the box that best completes each sentence.**

feet	need	deep	sea	real

1. I go with Mom to the _____ sea _____.

2. The water is not _____ deep _____.

3. I just got my _____ feet _____ wet.

4. I _____ need _____ my flip-flops, please.

5. There is _____ real _____ salt in the water.

SCHOOL-HOME CONNECTION Read the completed page with your child. Make a list of the words that are spelled with *ee* and a list of words spelled with *ea*.

Set Sail
Lesson 27   **59**

Name _____

▶ **Read the paragraph. Find the sentence that tells the main idea. Write it on the lines. Then write a title for the paragraph.** Answers may vary.

Title

_____

What Is in the Sea?
_____

Much more than water is in the sea. The sea is filled with living things. Many animals and plants live there. Some of the animals look like plants. We use many of the living things that are in the sea.

Main Idea

_____

The sea is filled with living things.

_____

_____

_____

_____

Set Sail
Lesson 27

SCHOOL-HOME CONNECTION Read a picture book with your child. Discuss the main idea of the story.

Harcourt

▶ **Write the word from the box that best completes each sentence.**

day	rain	say	pail	gray	play

1. It is a sunny _____ day _____.

2. What did you _____ say _____?

3. I have my _____ pail _____.

4. My friend wants to _____ play _____.

5. The sky turned _____ gray _____.

6. It's starting to _____ rain _____.

SCHOOL-HOME CONNECTION Ask your child to read the finished page to you. Then work together to list more words that contain the long vowel a sound spelled ay or ai.

Set Sail
Lesson 29 61

Harcourt

▶ **Choose the word that finishes each sentence. Write it on the line.**

plan   planned   planning

1. I had _____ planned _____ to go to bed.

wagged   wag   wagging

2. My dog was _____ wagging _____ his tail.

tapped   tap   tapping

3. Who is _____ tapping _____ at the door?

hugging   hug   hugged

4. I _____ hugged _____ my grandma at the door.

SCHOOL-HOME CONNECTION Ask your child to read the completed page to you. Together, write sentences for some of the answer words not used.

Harcourt

Name _____

▶ **Complete each contraction pair.**

1. I have

_____

- - - - - - - - - - - - - - - - -

I've

2. They had

_____

- - - - - - - - - - - - - - - - -

They'd

3. You have

_____

- - - - - - - - - - - - - - - - -

You've

4. You are

_____

- - - - - - - - - - - - - - - - -

You're

5. We have

_____

- - - - - - - - - - - - - - - - -

We've

6. We are

_____

- - - - - - - - - - - - - - - - -

We're

 TRY THIS Write two sentences about things you can explore at the beach. Use two or more contractions in your sentences.

SCHOOL-HOME CONNECTION On index cards or small pieces of paper, write each word pair and each contraction. You and your child hold the cards like playing cards. Try to match word pairs and contractions. The player with the most pairs wins.

Harcourt

Name _____

▶ **Finish each sentence. Choose the correct word that has the same vowel sound as the underlined word. Circle the word and write it.**

feather
(bread)
meat

1. I <u>fed</u> the bird. I gave it some

_____

- - - - - - - - - - - - - - - -

bread .

meal
(breakfast)
breath

2. I like to <u>help</u>. Today I made

_____

- - - - - - - - - - - - - - - -

breakfast .

breakfast
heat
(weather)

3. I'll go with <u>them</u> even in bad

_____

- - - - - - - - - - - - - - - -

weather .

(instead)
real
head

4. I sleep in my <u>bed</u>.
My bird rests on the sand

_____

- - - - - - - - - - - - - - - -

instead .

SCHOOL-HOME CONNECTION Have your child
explain how he or she chose the answers.

Harcourt

Name _____

▶ **Write go or went to complete each sentence. Then circle now or in the past to show when each action took place.**

1. You and I can _____go_____ to the zoo.

(now)

in the past

2. We _____went_____ last month.

now

(in the past)

3. We can _____go_____ again.

(now)

in the past

4. The baboons _____went_____ from rock to rock last time.

now

(in the past)

 TRY THIS Work with a partner to change the sentences. If it is in the past, make it tell about now. If it is about now, make it tell about something in the past. Use the words go and went.

SCHOOL-HOME CONNECTION Share the completed page with your child. If he or she is confused about the terms "now" and "in the past," substitute the terms "today" and "yesterday."

Set Sail
Lesson 31   65

▶ **Fill in the words in the box to finish each sentence. Then do what the sentences tell you to do.**

disappear   ground   across   mouth   shook

1. The baboon likes to _____ disappear _____

   in the tall grass. Draw a circle around her.

2. A hippo is resting in the pond, not on the

   _____ ground _____. Color the hippo gray.

3. The crocodile walks _____ across _____ the

   mud. Color the mud black.

Harcourt

4. The gazelle opens her _____mouth_____ for a drink. Color the water blue.

5. The bird _____shook_____ his wings to get the water off. Draw drops of water coming off the bird.

▶ **Find each word in the puzzle. Circle it. Words go across only.**

s	h	o	o	k	f	r	l	b	n
d	i	s	a	p	p	e	a	r	b
c	h	r	n	p	m	o	u	t	h
a	g	n	g	r	o	u	n	d	y
o	a	v	a	c	r	o	s	s	i

TRY THIS Write a newspaper headline for the animal picture on page 66. Use the words <u>disappear</u> and <u>across</u>.

SCHOOL-HOME CONNECTION Ask your child to share the completed pages with you. Discuss what he or she marked on the picture on page 66.

Set Sail
Lesson 32   67

▶ **Read the sentences. Do what they tell you. Circle the words that have the same vowel sound as <u>bread</u>.**

What Is Up Ahead?

1. It has (feathers.) Color the (feathers) blue.

2. Its (web) is (spread) between the branches. Color it (red.)

3. It is (heavy) and has a huge (head.) Color it gray.

4. It looks like bad (weather.) Circle the storm clouds.

5. A crocodile is taking a bath. Color it green.

TRY THIS | Make funny or scary warning signs. Each one should include the word <u>ahead</u>.

SCHOOL-HOME CONNECTION Share the completed page with your child. Find the words with the short *e* sound spelled *ea*. Work together to make up new sentences for those words.

Harcourt

Name _____

▶ **Read the words in the box. Then write
the correct word in each sentence.**

bread	Get	head	led	ready

1. _____ the _____ !
   Get   bread

2. We are _____ .
           ready

3. Watch your _____ !
               head

4. Who _____ the ants here?
       led

SCHOOL-HOME CONNECTION Read over the completed page with
your child. Then help him or her think of more words with the short
e sound in *head* or *get*.

Set Sail
Lesson 32   **69**

Name _____

▶ **Think about what Baboon learned about the world. Then finish the web.** Answers may vary.

big

hot

The world is _____ .

soft

dark

SCHOOL-HOME CONNECTION Ask your child to read the answers he or she wrote to complete the page. Discuss why Baboon gave so many answers.

Harcourt

Name _____

▶ **Complete the sentences. Use the words in the box. Write each word on a line.**

arm	far	part	start	yard

1. How _____far_____ does the world go?

2. You _____start_____ right here.

3. Stretch out your _____arm_____.

4. I can reach your _____yard_____.

5. That is the best _____part_____.

TRY THIS Where in the world would you like to go most? Write a sentence or draw a picture that tells about the place.

SCHOOL-HOME CONNECTION Ask your child to read you the completed page. Then have him or her use the words *far* and *yard* in sentences.

Harcourt

Name _____

▶ **Read what Baboon says. Circle the pictures and words he is talking about.**

1. **These things are hot.**

fire   steam   ice cream   sun

2. **These things are hard.**

pillow   ice   bricks   wood

3. **These things are crunchy.**

popcorn   toast   water   leaves

4. **These things are heavy.**

bowling ball   feather   truck   hippo

Harcourt

TRY THIS Make a list of things you can find or think of that are light.

SCHOOL-HOME CONNECTION Share the completed page with your child. Ask him or her to think of more things that are heavy, crunchy, hard, or hot.

Name _____

▶ **Complete each sentence. Write the word on the line.**

JUNGLE REPORT — MAY 1ST

spotting   spotted   spot
_____

1. We have __*spotted*__ a chimpanzee family.

patted   pat   patting
_____

2. They are __*patting*__ and cleaning each other.

stepped   stepping   step
_____

3. One baby chimp __*stepped*__ right up to us.

patting   pat   patted
_____

4. I __*patted*__ his hand.

nap   napping   napped
_____

5. Now he is __*napping*__. What a find!

SCHOOL-HOME CONNECTION Take turns creating sentences using *-ed* and *-ing*. Discuss the different meanings of the sentences depending upon the tense.

Harcourt

Name _____

▶ **Write the word that best completes each sentence.** Answers may vary.

| planet | spacecraft | rocket | space | pictures |

1. I wonder what's in _____ space _____ .

2. Saturn is a _____ planet _____ with rings.

3. The _____ rocket _____ lifted off the ground.

4. Stars and planets are in _____ space _____ .

5. The _____ spacecraft _____ flew to the satellite.

6. The satellite takes _____ pictures _____ .

Harcourt

Name _____

▶ **Read the words in the box. Put them in the chart. You can use the words more than once.** Answers may vary.

pictures	sun	stars	spacecraft	planet
moon	rocket		telescope	shuttle

Things in Space

sun
stars
planet
moon

Things We Can See from Earth

sun
stars
moon

Ways to Travel in Space

spacecraft
rocket
shuttle

Things That Help Us Learn About Space

pictures
telescope

Harcourt

SCHOOL-HOME CONNECTION Discuss space exploration during your lifetime with your child. Explain that rockets preceded the space shuttle program.

Name _____

▶ **Write the word on the line that best completes each sentence.**

| cold | So | ago | go | old |

1. The first trip to space took place over
_____

40 years _____ago_____ .

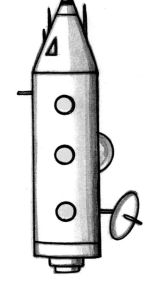

2. Space is very _____cold_____ .

3. Those who _____go_____ up are brave.

4. John Glenn was 77 years _____old_____
when he made his second trip.

5._____So_____ would you go if you could?

TRY THIS Pretend you are looking at Earth from space. Write a sentence describing what you see.

SCHOOL-HOME CONNECTION Ask your child to list other words that have the long *o* sound.

Harcourt

Name _____

▶ **Think about what you read. Fill in the chart.** Responses will vary.

Planets

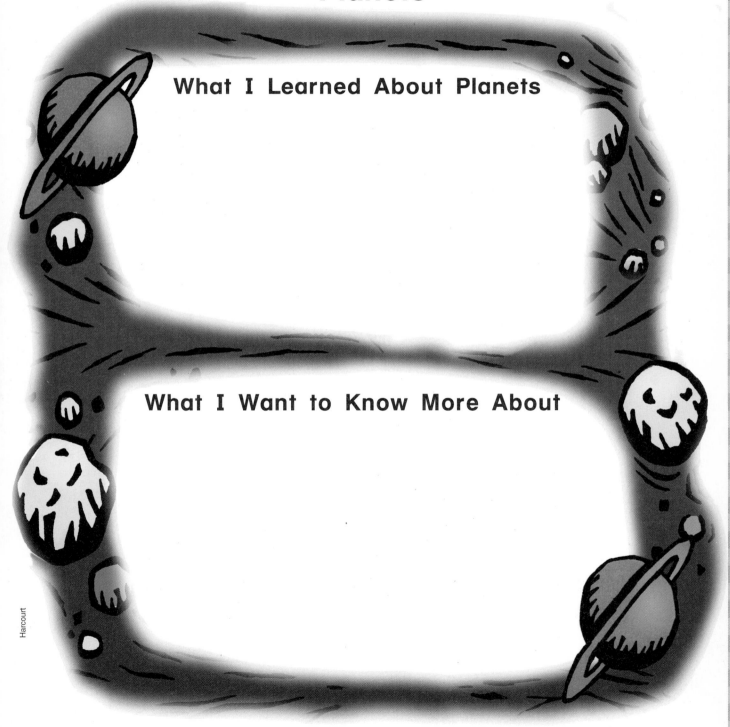

What I Learned About Planets

What I Want to Know More About

SCHOOL-HOME CONNECTION Ask your child to read you the completed page. Ask him or her what fact was the most interesting or surprising.

Set Sail
Lesson 36   77

Harcourt

Name _____

▶ **Write the word to finish each sentence.**

isn't   don't   hasn't

_____

1. The spacecraft _____ *hasn't* _____
   landed yet.

aren't   isn't   don't

_____

2. We _____ *don't* _____ have long
   until we reach Mars.

3. Mars has two moons, but they

don't   isn't   aren't

_____

_____ *aren't* _____ very big.

don't   hasn't   doesn't

_____

4. Mars _____ *doesn't* _____ have water.

TRY THIS Make two lists. Call one list "Things I Like" and the other list "Things I Don't Like." Which list is longer?

SCHOOL-HOME CONNECTION Work with your child to think of sentences that use the words *doesn't* and *don't.*

Harcourt

Name _____

▶ **Write the word that best completes each line of the invitation.**

| bright | light | night | right | might |

A Star-Gazing Party!

Where: Cindy's house

_____

When: Tuesday _____ night _____ at 8 o'clock.

_____

Please bring a flash_____ light _____. Venus should

_____

be _____ bright _____ at sunset. If there are no

_____

clouds, we _____ might _____ see Mars.

_____

Please come _____ right _____ on time!

Cindy
555-1133

SCHOOL-HOME CONNECTION Play a game with your child. Write the word *right*. Under that word, write *bright*. Ask your child to tell you what letter you added. Repeat with the words *might*, *light*, *night*, and *sight*, asking your child to tell you what letter you changed.

Set Sail
Lesson 37

Harcourt

Name _____

▶ **Read the clues. Write the words to complete the puzzle.**

cold	fold	most	roll	hold

1.
h
o
2.
c
3. r o l l
d
4.
m l
5. f o l d
s
t

Across

3. do this with a ball

5. make something small and neat

Down

1. keep something in your hand

2. not hot

4. greatest amount

Set Sail
Lesson 37

SCHOOL-HOME CONNECTION Work with your child to write a sentence for each of the Spelling Words.

Harcourt

Name _____

▶ **Read the paragraph. Circle the main idea and write four details about the paragraph on the rocks.**

(In 1997, people learned a lot about Mars from a robot.) A robot car called Rover traveled to Mars. The Rover's job was to collect facts about Mars. The Rover picked up rocks. It took pictures. It collected facts about the weather on Mars.

Things the Rover Did

collected information about Mars

took pictures

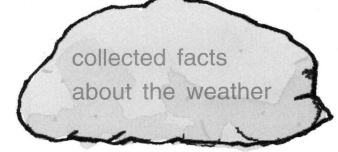
collected facts about the weather

picked up rocks

TRY THIS Use the main idea to make up a title for the paragraph.

SCHOOL-HOME CONNECTION Read newspaper captions with your child. Discuss photos and captions.

Set Sail
Lesson 37   **81**

Harcourt

Name _____

► **Complete each sentence. Write the word on the lines.**

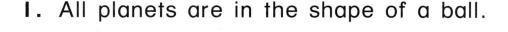

| huge | mule | cube | tune | use |

1. All planets are in the shape of a ball.

_____

Not one is a ____cube____.

2. Planets are very, very big.

_____

Planets are ____huge____.

3. So far, we see no life on other planets.

_____

A ____mule____ could not live on Pluto.

4. Spacecraft run on batteries.

_____

These ____use____ the sun's light for power.

5. There is no air in space, so it is silent.

_____

If you play a ____tune____, no one will hear.

Set Sail
Lesson 39

 **SCHOOL-HOME CONNECTION** Ask your child to read to you the completed page. Discuss his or her answer choices.

Harcourt

Name _____

▶ **Circle the word that best completes each sentence. Write it on the line.**

small
smaller
(smallest)

1. Which planet _____ is the _____ smallest _____ of all?

smallest
small
(smaller)

2. The moon is _____ smaller _____ than Earth.

new
(newest)
newer

3. The _____ newest _____ telescope is called the Hubble Space Telescope.

oldest
old
(older)

4. Find out if this star is _____ older _____ than that star.

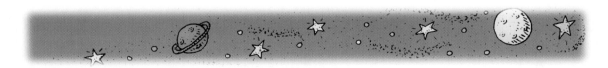

⟨TRY THIS⟩ Draw a picture to show these words: <u>long</u>, <u>longer</u>, <u>longest</u>.

 SCHOOL-HOME CONNECTION Use the words *big* and *small* to compare the sizes of familiar objects in the home.

Harcourt

Name _____

▶ **Find these words in the puzzle. Circle them. The words go across and down.**

| eat | treat | heat | neat | meat |

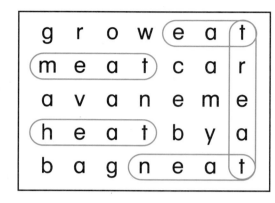

```
g  r  o  w  e  a  t
m  e  a  t  c  a  r
a  v  a  n  e  m  e
h  e  a  t  b  y  a
b  a  g  n  e  a  t
```

▶ **Complete each sentence.**

1. People in space have to ___eat___ .

2. They ___heat or eat___ special food.

3. Peanuts make a good ___treat___ .

4. Still, it is hard to stay ___neat___ .

5. Chicken and beef are two kinds of ___meat___ .

SCHOOL-HOME CONNECTION Ask your child to show you how he or she solved the word-search puzzle at the top of the page.

Harcourt

The Long Flight

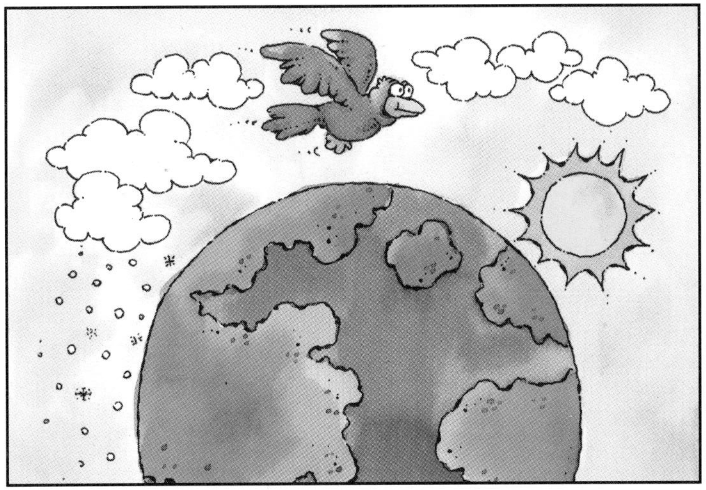

1

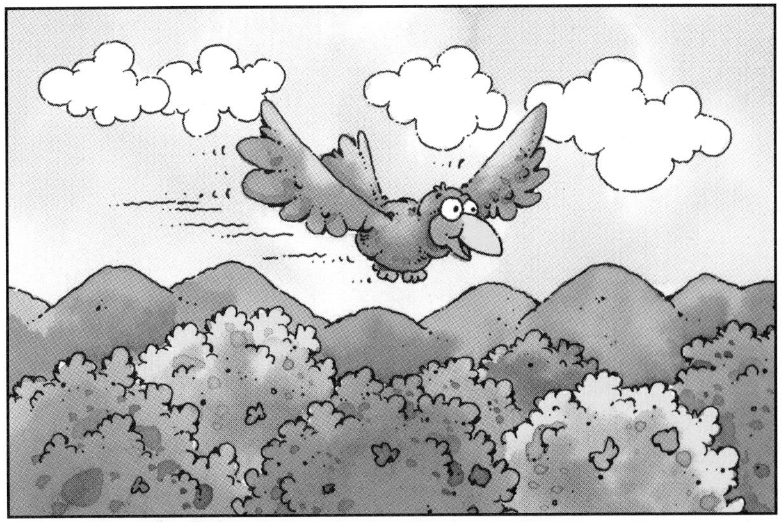

Fall came. Blue Bird
flew higher and higher.

3

Blue Bird flew a long time.
The sky got lighter and lighter.

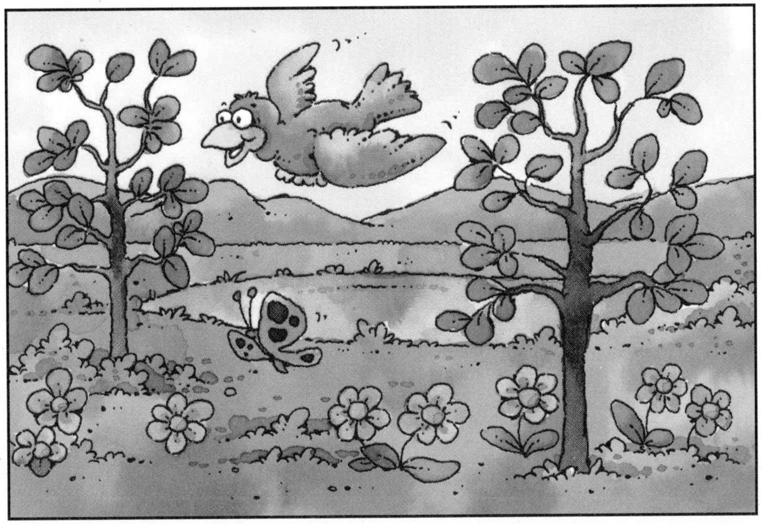

6

Blue Bird found a
wonderful warm home.

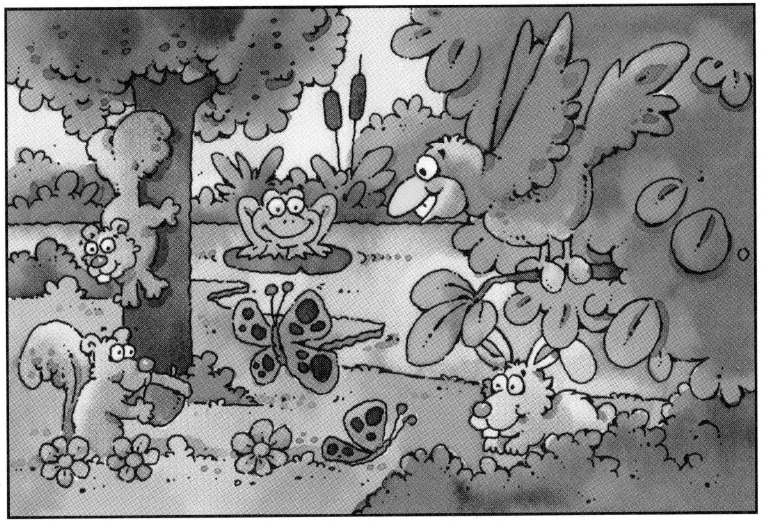

8

Fold

Fold

4

The winter grew chilly. Other birds joined him as he flew.

2

Blue Bird grew and grew.

Fold

Fold

Sometimes there was nothing to eat. Blue Bird was not afraid.

5

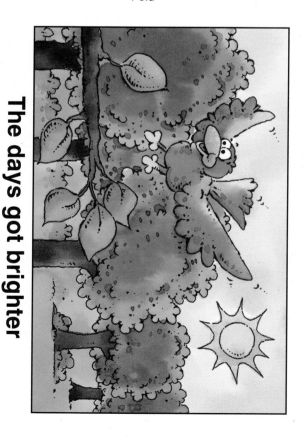

The days got brighter and brighter.

7

Frog and Mouse

— Fold —

Mouse could not stay and play. He had to work.

— Fold —

Then the two played near the woods.

8

"Make sure you get set for winter. Then you may play."

6

One gray night Frog wanted to play with Mouse.

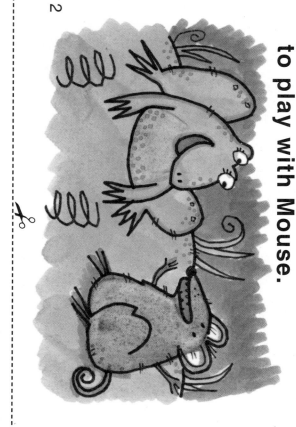

Winter was near. Mouse did not want to be caught in the cold without a home.

Fold

Fold

Frog helped Mouse until the job was finished.

His father had said, "Always find a winter home."

Find Something to Do

— Fold —

My tower crashes. My mom says, "Find something different to do."

— Fold —

How do you find something to do?

Of course I want to help. This is something to do.

On a rainy day my mom says,
"Find something to do."

We made the largest
cookies I've ever seen.

7

4

I run like a wild animal.
My mom says, "Listen child,
you need to mind."

"I need your help
with these cookies."

5

— Fold —

— Fold —

Crumbs in the Bed

1

Fold

"Do you want toast?" asked Jake.

3

Rover didn't stop. He ate both the jam and the toast. Now I have a bed full of crumbs!

8

Fold

Jake brought the toast. Rover had to see.

9

2

I am sick and in my bed.

Fold

4

"Yes, cold toast
with jam, please,"
I said.

Fold

Rover sniffed and jumped all
over the bed. "Stop!" I shouted. 7

Rover jumps on my bed.
I told him to stop jumping.

5

Three Little Moles

3 MOLES

"I'd be careful if I were you,"
he said. "On a clear day Snake
moves quietly in the grass."

Fold

Fold

Show the three moles
hiding in the hole.

"You're rude, Mule,"
said the little moles.

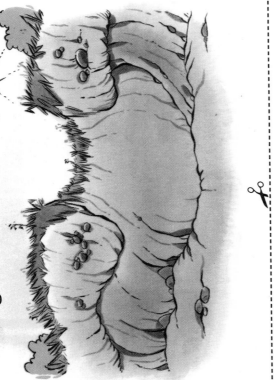

4

"We are not afraid," the moles said.

2

An old mule spotted three cute moles near the edge of a hole.

— Fold —

— Fold —

"I mean no harm to you. Go find a safe place to hide," said Mule. 7

The old mule said, "Snake can break out fast. He looks like a long tube."

5

If I went

to the Moon

Harcourt

— Fold —

If I could, I'd leave right now and fly straight there.

Harcourt

— Fold —

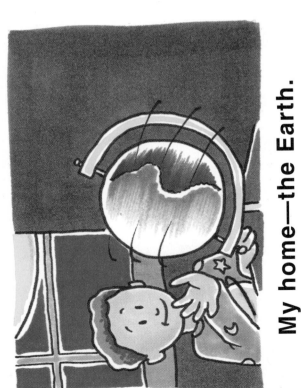

My home—the Earth.

When I got there, I'd put boots on my feet and take a walk. What would I see?

Set Sail
Cut-out Fold-up Book

I'd sleep and eat in space.

It's not easy to go to the moon.

— Fold —

I'd read all about the moon. 5

7

— Fold —

THE RACE

The baboon led the way.

Fold

Fold

Who do you think will win?

THE RACE

8

The crocodile's head slipped under the water and disappeared.

6

Set Sail
Cut-out Fold-up Book

2

Get ready. Get set. Go!

The gazelle is ahead now. 7

— Fold —

4

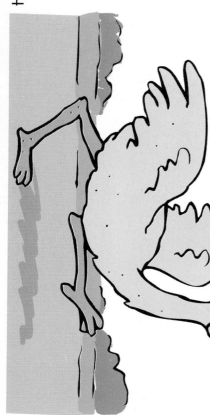

The ostrich spread her feathers and leaped into the race.

— Fold —

The rhinoceros ran across the meadow.

5

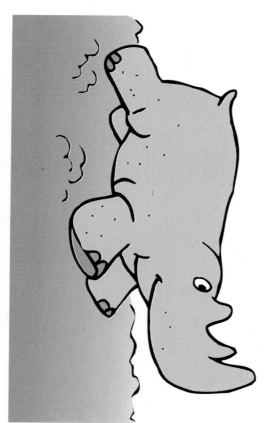

Cats
in Space

1

Fold

Fold

"Now that you are home, what
do you want to do first?"
"We want to roll on the ground."

9

3

"There you have it. Two
cats come home. So long
from B.D. Reporter."

8

✂

4

"It's very cold. I wouldn't
go there again."

"Welcome home. What is
it like on Pluto?"

2

"Hello. Two cats flew to
Pluto in a rocket. In just
a moment we will ask
them about their trip
to this cold planet."

— Fold — — Fold —

5

7

Skills and Strategies Index

Skills and Strategies Index